Social Work and Dementia

Social Work and Dementia

DAVID MOORE
AND
KIRSTY JONES

Series Editors: Jonathan Parker and Greta Bradley

LEARNING
RESOURCES
CENTRE

HAVERING COLLEGE

$SAGE | LearningMatters

Los Angeles | London | New Delhi
Singapore | Washington DC

362·19683   Q   189587

Learning Matters
An imprint of SAGE Publications Ltd
1 Oliver's Yard
55 City Road
London EC1Y 1SP

SAGE Publications Inc.
2455 Teller Road
Thousand Oaks, California 91320

SAGE Publications India Pvt Ltd 150
B 1/I 1 Mohan Cooperative Industrial Area
Mathura Road
New Delhi 110 044

SAGE Publications Asia-Pacific Pte Ltd
3 Chuch Street
#10–04 Samsung Hub
Singapore 049483

Editor: Luke Block
Development Editor: Kate Lodge
Production Controller: Chris Marke
Project Management: Deer Park Productions,
Tavistock, Devon
Marketing Manager: Tamara Navaratnam
Cover Design: Code 5
Typeset by: Pantek Media, Maidstone, Kent
Printed by: TJ International Ltd, Padstow, Cornwall

Library of Congress Control Number: 2012936241

British Library Cataloguing in Publication Data

A catalogue record for this book is available from the British Library

ISBN: 978 0 85725 839 7
ISBN: 978 0 85725 621 8 (pbk)

Contents

Willem van der Valk, a member of the HOPE group.

Les Pepper, a member of the HOPE group.

The HOPE group are a group of people living with dementia who believe that through sharing their direct experience, they can provide insight into how people can live well with dementia.

They are passionate about challenging the current perspective of dementia and demonstrating the positive experience of living with dementia. This is reflected in the group's name, which is an acronym for Hope Of People with Experience.

About the authors

David Moore is a Senior Lecturer and the Education Lead at the Association for Dementia Studies (ADS). ADS was established in 2009 at the University of Worcester under the leadership of Professor Dawn Brooker. It is a multiprofessional group of educationalists, researchers and practitioners who are expert in the field of person-centred dementia care and support. David joined ADS from West Sussex County Council where he worked for four years developing self-directed support, service involvement for people living with dementia and the HOPE group. This is a group of people living with dementia involved in developing awareness among professionals and the public about the lived experience of dementia. Before this he worked as the chief assessor for a national qualification in dementia care. David has also managed a number of services for people with dementia, including Merevale House care home which was featured on BBC TV's *Can Gerry Robinson Fix Dementia Care Homes?* David also worked for Dementia Care Matters Ltd for four years.

Kirsty Jones is a Learning and Development Officer working at West Sussex County Council and is the lead for Older People's Mental Health and Dementia Care learning and development. Kirsty works across a number of social and health care settings providing opportunities to develop knowledge and enhance practical skills to support people with dementia to live well and free from discrimination. She has been responsible for the implementation of Dementia Care Mapping (DCM) within West Sussex County Council day services, a fundamental project that is aiding the development into specialist dementia services. Kirsty now supports the HOPE group in developing the innovative work that David started. Prior to this Kirsty has worked within domiciliary care, co-ordinating services for older people living with dementia in their own homes. Kirsty has recently completed a diploma-level qualification in person-centred dementia care provided by Dementia Care Matters.

Acknowledgements

We would like to acknowledge a number of people without whose support this book would not have been produced. They include Kirsty, Daisy and Amber-Marie Moore for their words of encouragement and understanding; Martin, Daisy-May and Ella Jones for their continued patience and reassurance; members of the HOPE group, including Les and Audrey Pepper, Christine and Willem van der Valk, Graham Browne, Bob and Marilyn Noble, who provided inspirational learning; the staff at the Association for Dementia Studies, the University of Worcester, including Professor Dawn Brooker, Dr Karan Jutlla, Kate Read, Helen Cain and Jenny La Fontaine; and the dedicated staff and customers of West Sussex County Council Adults' Services, Wolverhampton City Council and Worcestershire County Council.

Finally, we would like to thank Emy Lou Harris for allowing us to use the photographs in this book. (www.emylouphotography.co.uk)

Foreword

It is through my involvement with education and training for those working with people with dementia across health and social care that I am able to highlight the valuable contribution that this book makes within this very important field. I am a lecturer in dementia studies for the Association for Dementia Studies at the University of Worcester. The authors of this book are known well to me – in particular, David Moore with whom I work closely in delivering education and training for health professionals.

While we have made rapid changes that promote person-centred approaches to dementia care for the health and social care professionals through education and training, there is little scholarly guidance available that provides practical ways of working with people with dementia. Indeed social workers play a key role in supporting people with dementia to live well. This book has been produced not only to provide social workers (both students and professionals) with theoretical understandings of person-centred approaches to care, but also to encourage critical thinking and practical ways of working with such individuals.

There is a vast amount of literature which discusses the various models of practice in relation to dementia care. Government guidelines and policy in relation to people with dementia are too covered. However, what is missing in this literature is a discussion of the ways in which practitioners and professionals can use this information to help them support people to live well with dementia. The authors of this book, as a result of their professional backgrounds and experiences, have structured each chapter to link theory to practice.

In terms of content, the authors have particularly addressed those issues that have been seldom explored in the literature. For example, there is little research on the number of people with dementia who experience abuse. The authors have highlighted the potential challenges and complexities that may be faced by professionals when safeguarding people with dementia. As with all the chapters, readers are provided with current, up-to-date information in relation to that field; they are then provided with a number of case studies so that they are able to put that information into context; and then asked to work through a number of activities. These activities are designed to encourage critical thinking about their role as social workers and, based on their own expertise and knowledge, the authors provide possible suggestions for these activities.

This book is an excellent resource for both teaching and learning how to embody person-centred approaches to dementia care. It is also informative for those merely seeking knowledge about dementia care in relation to the various models of practice; current policy and practice; safeguarding; the personalisation agenda; and promoting independence in their homes for people with dementia. Based on this information, the authors also evaluate the future of dementia care, and encourage readers to consider how their roles as social workers can develop in order to fully meet the needs of people with dementia as well as fulfil the aims of the National Dementia Strategy. In my view, this easy-to-read, highly resourceful book should be core reading for both social work students and those practising within the field. It is also a useful resource for those providing education and training to promote person-centred approaches to dementia care. As a radical pedagogue, I am extremely pleased that this book promotes empowerment by encouraging social workers to think both critically and reflectively about their practice when working with people with dementia.

Dr Karan Jutlla
Lecturer in Dementia Studies
Association for Dementia Studies, University of Worcester

Series editors' preface

The Western world including the UK faces numerous challenges over forthcoming years, many of which are perhaps heightened following the 2007 fiscal crisis and its lasting ramifications. These include dealing with the impact of an increasingly ageing population, with its attendant social care needs, and working with the financial implications that such a changing demography brings. The ramifications of this for people with dementia are well rehearsed but still, to an extent, an unknown quantity. National and global perturbations have continued to influence and mould social and health policy developments, which often determine the ways in which they are applied in social work practice. This book adds to our knowledge of practice in those areas in which dementia is an issue.

Migration has increased as a global phenomenon and we now live and work with the implications of international issues in our everyday and local lives. Often these issues influence how we construct our social services and determine what services we need to offer. It is likely that as a social worker you will work with a diverse range of people throughout your career, many of whom have experienced significant, even traumatic, events that require a professional and caring response grounded, of course, in the laws and social policies that have developed as a result. As well as working with individuals, however, you may be required to respond to the needs of a particular community disadvantaged by world events or excluded within local communities because of assumptions made about them, and you may be embroiled in some of the tensions that arise from implementing policy-based approaches that may conflict with professional values. What is clear within these contexts is that you may be working with a range of people who are often at the margins of society, socially excluded or in need of protection and safeguarding: as people age and the incidences of dementia increase, you will require skills and knowledge as a social worker to deal with this wide range of life experiences that people with dementia and their carers have had. This text provides important knowledge and information to help you become aware of these issues, and to respond appropriately when faced with challenging situations.

Reflection, revision and reform allow us to focus clearly on what knowledge is useful to engage with in learning to be a social worker. The focus on 'statutory' social work and, by dint of that, involuntary clients, brings to the fore the need for social workers to be well-versed in the mechanisms and nuances of legislation that can be interpreted and applied to empower, protect and assist, but also to understand the social policy arena in which practice is forged. This important book provides readers with a beginning sense of the realities of practice and the importance of understanding the history and biographies of people with dementia and those around them, and the legal and policy landscape in which social workers practise. It also provides knowledge of the ways dementia impacts on the lives of individuals in the UK.

The books in this series respond to the agendas driven by changes brought about by professional body, government and disciplinary review. They aim to build on and offer introductory texts based on up-to-date knowledge and social policy development and to help communicate this in an accessible way, preparing the ground for future study as you develop your social work career. The books are written by people who are passionate about social work and social services and who aim to instil that passion in others. The knowledge introduced in this book is important for all social workers in all fields of practice as they seek to reaffirm social work's commitment to those it serves.

Professor Jonathan Parker, Bournemouth University
Greta Bradley, University of York

Introduction

Don't ignore me. I'm still human and that's it in a nutshell.

(Person with dementia)

The above quote illustrates the essence of working with people with dementia: remembering that each person with dementia is a unique individual who needs to have their humanity accepted and acknowledged. Social work is key to promoting this understanding through the empowerment of people with dementia and their carers. This empowerment can be achieved by having an awareness of current and relevant legislation, advocacy, joint working, re-ablement and personalisation of services.

Why there is a need for this book

Although there have been a number of documents exploring the issues concerning social work and dementia, including the excellent *Social work and people with dementia: Partnerships, practice and persistence* (2006) by Professor Mary Marshall and Margaret Anne Tibbs, it was felt that there was a need for a publication that would highlight the rapidly changing face of social work as a result of the personalisation agenda and how people with dementia can benefit from these developments. Consequently this book has been written to provide help and guidance for social work students and practitioners who are involved in the critical role of supporting people with dementia and their carers.

Content of the book

This book has been written with the support of staff and service users/customers of West Sussex County Council, Worcestershire County Council and Wolverhampton City Council. The information has then been used as the basis for the following chapters.

The first chapter introduces you to the different forms of dementia, including Alzheimer's disease, vascular dementia, dementia with Lewy bodies and the frontal–temporal dementias. The chapter moves on to ask you to consider how it may feel to live with dementia, as a way of creating a sense of empathy between yourself and those you work with. Next we discuss the different medications that can be used to slow the progression of some of the symptoms of dementia, followed by an examination of the use of antipsychotic medications. The final part of the chapter examines the different paradigms of dementia including the medical model, the social model and the enriched model.

Chapter 2 examines the various strategies and legislation relating to supporting people with dementia and their families. You will be introduced to the different objectives of the National Dementia Strategy which was published by the Department of Health in 2009 as guidance to improve services for people with dementia living in England. The chapter then explores another document produced by the Department of Health, *Nothing ventured, nothing gained*. You will see that this guidance explores the complexities of risk enablement for people who have dementia. The significance of the Mental Capacity Act (2005) will also be discussed, in particular the five key principles of the Act. You will be asked to consider how a person's capacity is assessed as well as contemplating the concept of best interests. Chapter 2 finishes by considering other pieces of legislation that are relevant in the support of people with dementia, including the Human Rights Act 1998.

Chapter 3 examines the critical issue of safeguarding people living with dementia. The different terminology used in safeguarding is explored to enable you to consider how language is developing as a consequence of the personalisation agenda. The roots of the current practices and ideas in safeguarding adults are identified, including the Department's of Health's *No secrets,* the NHS Community Care Act 1990, the Mental Capacity Act 2005 and the Human Rights Act 1998. You will be introduced to a number of concepts linked to this legislation, including proportionality. You will then consider the different pieces of research that have focused specifically on safeguarding people with dementia, including recent work by the Alzheimer's Society that focused on financial abuse of people with dementia.

Chapter 4 demonstrates how the personalisation agenda is being used to transform social care, in particular through the process of self-directed support. The benefits of this for people with dementia will be explored as well as the possible obstacles people with dementia may face. You will be asked to reflect upon why social work needs to become personalised, to consider the language used in the new world of personalisation and how you can enable personal budgets to work for people with dementia and their carers.

Chapter 5 introduces the concept of re-ablement and telecare and illustrates how these systems can help people living with dementia to stay in their own homes for longer, an aim reported by many people with dementia. You will be asked to consider the benefits of such services and the role of other professionals within these services. Furthermore, the ethical considerations of the use of assistive technology will be examined as well as its potential benefits.

In the final chapter, the future of dementia care is explored and the role of social work within this is discussed. The chapter provides case examples of services that are currently in development in areas such as early diagnosis and intervention, carer support, hospital discharge, community support and end-of-life care.

How to use the book

This book has been written to be interactive. In each chapter there are a number of activities and questions that have been written to enable you to consider and reflect upon how the topics described can influence your current and future practice. You are asked to take responsibility for your learning which is aimed at developing your practice and your knowledge of how to support people living with dementia.

We strongly believe that in your role as a social worker you have the skills and abilities to enable people with dementia and their families to continue to lead fulfilling and worthwhile lives despite the diagnosis of dementia. Our aim is that this book will show you ways that this can be done and we hope you find it useful and relevant.

The Professional Capabilities Framework for Social Workers in England

This book has been carefully mapped to the new Professional Capabilities Framework for Social Workers in England and will help you to develop the appropriate standards at the right level. These standards are:

- **Professionalism**

  Identify and behave as a professional social worker committed to professional development.

- **Values and ethics**

  Apply social work ethical principles and values to guide professional practice.

- **Diversity**

  Recognise diversity and apply anti-discriminatory and anti-oppressive principles in practice.

- **Justice**

  Advance human rights and promote social justice and economic well-being.

- **Knowledge**

  Apply knowledge of social sciences, law and social work practice theory.

- **Judgement**

  Use judgement and authority to intervene with individuals, families and communities to promote independence, provide support and prevent harm, neglect and abuse.

- **Critical reflection and analysis**

  Apply critical reflection and analysis to inform and provide a rationale for professional decision-making.

- **Contexts and organisations**

  Engage with, inform, and adapt to changing contexts that shape practice. Operate effectively within your own organisational frameworks and contribute to the development of services and organisations. Operate effectively within multi-agency and interprofessional settings.

- **Professional leadership**

    Take responsibility for the professional learning and development of others through supervision, mentoring, assessing, research, teaching, leadership and management.

References to these standards will be made throughout the text and you will find a diagram of the professional capabilities framework in Appendix 1.

Chapter 1

An introduction to dementia and person-centred care

Introduction

Dementia has in recent years become a high priority for health and social care. In 2007 the Alzheimer's Society commissioned a report entitled *Dementia UK: Report to the Alzheimer's Society* that explored the prevalence and economic cost of dementia (Knapp *et al.*, 2007). The report estimated that there were 683,597 people with dementia in the UK. In the same year the National Audit Office also produced a report focusing on the need to improve services and support for people with dementia. One of the notable conclusions of this latter report is that 'dementia presents a significant and urgent challenge to health and social care in terms of both numbers of people affected and cost'. (Bourn *et al.*, 2007, p11). Consequently in 2009 *Living well with dementia: A national dementia strategy* was published. This is the Department of Health's five-year strategy outlining its plans for improving health and social care services for people with dementia and their carers (Department of Health, 2009a). The strategy clearly demonstrates the government's commitment to improving the lives of people with dementia. The strategy notes that by 2038 there will be 1.4 million people living with dementia in the UK.

Chapter 2 explores the role of social work in supporting the objectives of the National Dementia Strategy. The All-Party Parliamentary Group on Dementia highlighted in their inquiry into improving lives through cost-effective dementia services that 'it is well known that dementia is a significant and growing driver of demand for health and social care' (All-Party Parliamentary Group on Dementia, 2011, p9). A person with dementia may be receiving support from a range of services. The inquiry also highlighted the observation by the Commission on funding of care and support in England that even though people with dementia have a physical disease of the brain they are not always eligible to receive NHS-funded care and much of the care is provided by care staff from social services. Therefore as a social worker your role will be fundamental in supporting people with dementia to identify their care needs and assist in establishing how these needs can be met. Developing your knowledge of dementia and the principles of person-centred care will enable you to understand how people with dementia can be supported to continue to live well and overcome some of the challenges associated with living with the condition.

In this chapter you will identify some of the common types of dementia and the signs and symptoms that can accompany these conditions. Alongside this you will also look at the prescribing and use of two different groups of medicine for people with dementia.

The chapter will also look at the different models and approaches to dementia care. You will consider the term 'person-centred care' and reflect on the theories behind this approach.

This chapter will help readers to:

- be aware of some of the different types of dementia;

- consider the signs and symptoms that are associated with dementia;

- identify two different groups of medicine prescribed to people with dementia;

- compare the different theoretical models of dementia care;

- reflect upon the major approaches and theories associated with 'person-centred care';

- be aware of tools used to evaluate the experience of living with dementia in care settings.

What is dementia?

The Mental Health Foundation defines dementia as . . . *a decline in mental ability which affects memory, thinking, problem-solving, concentration and perception.* (Mental Health Foundation 2012).

Each individual's experience of dementia will of course be unique. However, the following section aims to provide you with an overview of some of the most common causes of dementia and the associated symptoms.

Dementia is not a condition or illness in itself. It is a term used to describe a number of conditions or illnesses that affect a person's brain functioning and cause them to experience a decline in their cognitive skills. This decline in cognitive skills causes a person to experience a number of symptoms including:

- problems with short-term memory;

- problems with thinking skills;

- problems with communication.

There are many different types of dementia. However, some are more common than others, as illustrated in Table 1.1.

Table 1.1 Some common types of dementia

Type of dementia	% of people with dementia with the condition
Alzheimer's disease	62%
Vascular dementia	17%
Mixed (Alzheimer's and vascular)	10%
Dementia with Lewy bodies	4%
Fronto-temporal	2%
Other	6%

(Estimate from Knapp *et al.*, 2007)

ACTIVITY **1.1**

Consider the key benefits of developing your knowledge of the most common types of dementia. How will this knowledge support you in your role as a social worker.

COMMENT

A person's experience of living with dementia will be unique and each individual's experience will be different. However, developing an understanding of some of the symptoms a person may experience can be helpful when supporting people with dementia to identify their care needs. As a social worker, knowing which type of dementia a person is living with will ensure that you can adapt your approach appropriately and identify with some of the challenges that the individual may be faced with as a result of the symptoms they may be experiencing.

Alzheimer's disease

Alzheimer's is a progressive disease, which means that gradually, over time, more parts of the brain are damaged. As this happens, the symptoms become more severe (Alzheimer's Society, 2011a).

In 1906 a German neurologist named Alois Alzheimer observed a patient, Frau Auguste D, who displayed strange behavioural symptoms including short-term memory loss. After Frau Auguste died, Alzheimer examined her brain and identified that amyloidal plaques (dead or dying cells and proteins) and neurofibrillary tangles (twisted protein) had developed in the normally empty spaces between nerve cells. These plaques and tangles attack the nerve and brain cells. As a result, some of these cells are damaged and therefore do not work as effectively while other cells are completely destroyed. This leads to deterioration in an individual's cognitive abilities. Nevertheless, it has been identified in people with Alzheimer's disease that not all of the brain is affected by these plaques and tangles and many areas of the brain will continue to function. It has also been discovered that people with Alzheimer's disease have a reduced amount of a chemical neurotransmitter called acetylcholine. This chemical is responsible for memory function.

The damage caused by the plaques and tangles and the reduction of acetylcholine in the brain causes the person with Alzheimer's disease to experience some of the following symptoms:

- short-term memory loss (however, long-term memory remains intact for some time);

- problems with communication;

- problems with reading and writing.

There is currently very little understanding of why these plaques and tangles develop in some people's brains and not in others. However, research continues to look into this essential area to develop knowledge and hopefully find a cure.

CASE STUDY

Mrs Hobbs has been living at home on her own following the death of her husband two years ago. Mrs Hobbs' family visit her on a regular basis and have recently noticed that she has become forgetful. Although her daughter, Mrs Sherwell, has phoned to tell her mother that she is coming round to see her at a specific time, when she arrives Mrs Hobbs is surprised to see her and can't recall having a phone conversation with her daughter. Mrs Hobbs's next-door neighbour stopped Mrs Sherwell on her way out one day and mentioned that she had bumped into Mrs Hobbs's in the high street recently and found her very confused and upset. She had asked her neighbour if she could take her back home.

Vascular dementia

Vascular dementia occurs when there is an interruption of the blood flow to the brain. A good blood supply is essential for carrying oxygen and nutrients to the brain in order to help it function. This crucial supply of oxygen is carried in the blood via the vascular system. If the vascular system becomes damaged or blocked, oxygen cannot get to the brain. Brain cells can then die, causing damage to the brain and resulting in the symptoms of dementia.

Alzheimer Scotland (2002) have identified various types of vascular dementia including the following:

- Arteriosclerotic dementia, which results from a reduced oxygen supply to the brain (chronic ischaemia).

- Vascular dementia that follows a stroke. Major strokes can be fatal or may lead to physical disability or vascular dementia due to damage to the brain.

- Multi-infarct dementia (MID), which develops gradually following a number of mini strokes or transient ischaemic attacks, which the person may not realise they are having. MID affects the cerebral cortex, which is the outer part of the brain.

- Subcortical vascular dementia (Binswanger's disease), which involves vascular damage to the nerve cell fibres of the inner parts of the brain (deep white matter) by affecting the sheath which insulates nerve fibres in the brain (demyelination).

- There is also a vascular dementia that involves both cortical and subcortical damage to the brain.

There are rarer causes of vascular dementia, which may affect some people with autoimmune inflammatory diseases that affect the arteries, such as systemic lupus erythematosus (SLE or lupus) and temporal arteritis (Alzheimer's Scotland, 2002).

The risk factors for vascular dementia are the same as those associated with strokes: high blood pressure (hypertension); diabetes; high cholesterol level; and heart disease (Alzheimers Scotland, 2002).

Symptoms of vascular dementia will vary depending on the location of the damage within the brain. A person with vascular dementia can develop symptoms quickly and it is often described as developing unexpectedly. While some of the symptoms are similar to those of other types of dementia, people with vascular dementia will experience specific symptoms related to this type of dementia. In particular it is thought that there is a link between the symptoms of depression and vascular dementia. Other symptoms of vascular dementia include:

- problems maintaining concentration;

- slurred speech;

- stroke-related symptoms.

CASE STUDY

Mr Kus is 74 years old and lives at home alone. About six months ago he had a small stroke. Since then he has been managing at home with regular visits from home care. Mr Kus's morning carer has reported that over the past week he has appeared to have problems concentrating and is finding it difficult to follow conversations. In addition his speech has become slurred and he seems less interested in completing his jigsaw, an activity he normally loves to engage with.

5

Dementia with Lewy bodies

Dementia with Lewy bodies (DLB) is a form of dementia that shares characteristics with both Alzheimer's and Parkinson's diseases. Dementia with Lewy bodies is sometimes referred to by other names, including Lewy body dementia, Lewy body variant of Alzheimer's disease, diffuse Lewy body disease, cortical Lewy body disease and senile dementia of Lewy body type. All these terms refer to the same disorder. (Alzheimer's Society, 2010a).

In 1912 Dr Frederic Lewy identified tiny protein deposits within the nerve cells in the brain stem. These protein deposits attack a chemical called dopamine. The resulting lack of dopamine causes the symptoms of Parkinson's disease such as problems with motor control. The proteins can increase and spread to other parts of the brain and attack chemical neurotransmitters called acetylcholine. This produces similar effects to those of Alzheimer's disease and therefore can cause a person to experience symptoms of this disease such as short-term memory loss. Other symptoms can include:

- visual hallucinations;

- delusions;

- fluctuating abilities.

In some cases people who have a diagnosis of Parkinson's disease can develop dementia similar to that of dementia with Lewy bodies.

CASE STUDY

John was diagnosed with Parkinson's disease at the age of 68 and manages the disease through various medications. John is now 76 years old and his son Paul is worried that his dad's condition is deteriorating. Following a recent visit, Paul has decided to move in temporarily with John as John has been talking about animals coming out of the TV and people in the street wanting his house as it has a bigger driveway.

Fronto-temporal dementia

The term 'fronto-temporal dementia' covers a range of conditions, including Pick's disease, frontal lobe degeneration, and dementia associated with motor neurone disease. All are caused by damage to the frontal lobe and/or the temporal parts of the brain. These areas are responsible for our behaviour, emotional responses and language skills (Alzheimer's Society, 2010b).

This particular type of dementia affects the front part of the brain, which is responsible for managing our social behaviour, therefore many of the symptoms of fronto-temporal dementia are linked to personality and behavioural changes. A person's memory will not be affected until later in the experience of dementia.

The most common form of fronto-temporal dementia is Pick's disease, named after Arnold Pick, who first discovered the disease in 1892. He identified abnormal bodies and cells that had developed inside nerve cells within the brain. These Pick bodies and cells contain an irregular protein called tau. In people with Pick's disease there is an increased amount of this type of protein in the frontal and temporal lobe of the brain.

Some of the symptoms of fronto-temporal dementia include:

* a loss of inhibition;

* a change in personality, i.e. becoming more outgoing or more withdrawn;

* an inability to appreciate what is socially unacceptable behaviour; for example, making rude comments or jokes at inappropriate moments.

CASE STUDY

Mrs Cross is 56 years old and lives at home with her husband. She has always been a very polite and reserved lady. However, her husband has noticed that recently she has become more outspoken and seems to lack empathy. A close friend came to visit one day and Mrs Cross made various inappropriate comments regarding the friend's current relationship with her daughter. The friend later discussed this in private with Mr Cross and both agreed that such behaviour is completely out of character for Mrs Cross.

Other types of dementia

While these are the most common types of dementia there are a number of others that are less common. However, some of the symptoms are different from the types of dementia already discussed.

Korsakoff's syndrome

Korsakoff's syndrome is a brain disorder usually associated with heavy alcohol consumption over a long period (Alzheimer's Society, 2010c).

The main symptom of Korsakoff's is memory loss and in some cases it can affect long-term memories. Some of the other symptoms may include:

* problems in obtaining new information;

* problems learning new skills;

* changes in personality.

Creutzfeldt-Jakob disease (CJD)

Creutzfeldt-Jakob disease (CJD) is the best known of a group of diseases called prion disease, which affect a form of protein found in the central nervous system and cause dementia (Alzheimer's Society, 2010d).

The early symptoms of CJD may include:

- faltering memory;
- changes in mood;
- loss of interest in the surrounding world.

The experience for the individual

As previously discussed, the experience of dementia will vary for each individual. It is important to remember that although a person with dementia may be experiencing a loss in their cognitive functioning, they will nevertheless retain the ability to experience emotions and feelings. The following quotes from people with dementia give an insight into the personal experience of living with the condition and some of the challenges they are faced with.

> *Sometimes they think of you as if you are gaga and [speaking slowly] 'can you do this, can you do that?'*

> (person with dementia, quoted in Williamson, 2008)

Unfortunately the approach of others will always be a challenge for people with dementia. It could be argued that this approach is due to a lack of understanding of dementia. As a social worker your role will be key to ensuring that discrimination and stigma are challenged in order to improve the lived experience of dementia.

> *The only good thing with it was we knew something was wrong and we were prepared for the worst. So, like, obviously we got the worst, it wasn't that bad.*

> (person with dementia, quoted in Williamson, 2008)

A person's experience of living with dementia will be shaped by their personality and their ability to develop coping mechanisms. Supporting a person with dementia to develop these coping mechanisms could have a significant impact on their experience.

> *I was relieved really that what I was trying to convince people had been verified.*

> (person with dementia, quoted in Williamson, 2008)

For some people with dementia receiving a diagnosis can bring about a sense of relief.

> *I felt I had a shock . . . I just thought it can't be. I said it's for other people.*

> (person with dementia, quoted in Williamson, 2008)

> *The angst and anger that I went through during the diagnostic process . . . I could have actually gone and thumped people.*

> (person with dementia, quoted in Williamson, 2008)

Ensuring that the person receives ongoing support during this early diagnosis stage is key. Manthorpe and Iliffe (2009) argue that *a key professional task becomes the support of the person dealing with the impact of this news, and the exploration of support, possible treatment, or symptom relief.*

Drug treatments and dementia

While there is currently no cure for dementia, over recent years drugs have been developed that can help slow the progression of some of the symptoms. This group of drugs is commonly referred to as anti-dementia drugs.

Anti-dementia drugs

Anti-dementia drugs are also referred to as acetylcholinesterase inhibitors. Currently there are three medicines used to help treat some of the symptoms of Alzheimer's disease. These are:

- donepezil;
- rivastigmine;
- galantamine.

These drugs prevent an enzyme known as acetylcholinesterase from breaking down acetylcholine in the brain. Increased concentrations of acetylcholine lead to increased communication between the nerve cells that use acetylcholine as a chemical messenger, which may in turn temporarily improve or stabilise the symptoms of Alzheimer's disease (Alzheimer's Society, 2011b).

Memantine (Ebixa) is also prescribed to assist the symptoms of Alzheimer's. However, this drug works differently from the anti-dementia drugs. Memantine blocks a messenger chemical known as glutamate. Glutamate is released in excessive amounts when brain cells are damaged by Alzheimer's disease, and this causes the brain cells to be damaged further (Alzheimer's Society, 2011b).

NICE guidance

In 2007 the National Institute for Health and Clinical Excellence (NICE) issued guidance for the prescribing of anti-dementia drugs. It claimed that there was not enough evidence to support the cost implications of prescribing these drugs to people who were in the early and late experience of Alzheimer's disease. It advised that these drugs would only be beneficial to people who were in the moderate experience of Alzheimer's disease.

The Alzheimer's Society and many people with dementia and their carers campaigned for this guidance to be changed. Following the launch of a judicial review in January 2007 by one of the drug manufacturers the High Court ordered NICE to make changes to its guidance as it was decided that it breached disability and race discrimination law. However, this ruling did not include the use of these drugs for people in the early or mild stages of Alzheimer's disease.

In October 2010 NICE further reviewed its guidance on the prescribing of these drugs and, taking into account evidence submitted by the Alzheimer's Society, made changes to its guidance. This guidance was confirmed in January 2011 and now states that 'Donepezil, galantamine and rivastigmine are now recommended as options for managing mild as well as moderate Alzheimer's disease, and memantine is now recommended as an option for managing moderate Alzheimer's disease for people who cannot take acetylcholinesterase (AChE) inhibitors, and as an option for managing severe Alzheimer's disease' (NICE, 2011, p4).

Antipsychotic medicines

Antipsychotic medicines are a group of drugs that were produced to treat conditions that cause a person to experience psychosis, i.e. seeing and/or hearing things that are not real or true. The current licensed use of antipsychotic drugs is for the treatment of schizophrenia. Some examples of these types of drugs include:

- olanzapine;
- risperidone;
- haloperidol.

Some people with dementia may experience psychosis as a symptom of their dementia and the use of these drugs can be very beneficial. According to The Royal College of Psychiatrists they work by affecting dopamine – a chemical neurotransmitter that brain cells need in order to communicate with each other. Some parts of the dopamine system can become overactive and this seems to contribute towards producing hallucinations and delusions.

Some of the side effects of antipsychotic medications include drowsiness, fatigue, slowness and parkinsonism. Parkinsonism produces symptoms such as an increase in saliva, impaired body movements and muscle tightness.

In November 2009 the Department of Health commissioned Professor Sube Banerjee to produce a report on the use and adverse effects of antipsychotic medication for people with dementia in the UK (Banerjee, 2009). The report identified that 180,000 people with dementia are treated with antipsychotic medication per year.

ACTIVITY *1.3*

Identify reasons as to why so many people with dementia in care homes are prescribed antipsychotic medicines.

COMMENT

Due to the sedating effect of these drugs it has been suggested that they are more commonly used as a way of trying to manage those behaviours in people with dementia that other people find difficult, for example, aggression.

The report stated that only 36,000 people with dementia who are prescribed an antipsychotic will derive any benefit from the treatment; 1,620 will suffer cerebrovascular adverse events; and there are 1,800 deaths per year on top of those that would be expected in this frail population.

As a result the report made 11 recommendations aimed at reducing the use of antipsychotics to a level where the benefits outweigh the risks. Broadly, the report makes the following recommendations.

- People with dementia should receive antipsychotics only when they really need them. Reducing the use of antipsychotics in people with dementia should be a priority for the NHS.

- Care home staff should be given a curriculum to develop skills in non-pharmacological treatment of behavioural disorder in dementia.

- Care homes could be assessed based on their use of antipsychotic medications and the availability of staff who are skilled in non-pharmacological management of behavioural and psychological symptoms in dementia.

- Psychological therapy resources should be made available for people with dementia and their carers.

- Further research should be carried out, including studies of non-pharmacological methods of treating behavioural problems in dementia and of alternative pharmacological treatments.

(Banerjee, 2009)

CASE STUDY

Mr Meaby attended a day service with nursing support once a week. Upon his arrival at the day service he was agitated, distressed and behaved aggressively towards the staff at the centre. He was prescribed Risperdal on an as required basis. It was decided that Mr Meaby should be given this medication by his wife before he came to the centre to alleviate his symptoms and help to calm him. Mrs Meaby was not happy with this approach and started to take her husband to a different day service. Here it seemed that the approach of the staff and the environment of the new day service meant that Mr Meaby no longer required the Risperdal.

Prevalence rates and economic effects of dementia

RESEARCH SUMMARY

In 2010 the Health Economics Research Centre at the University of Oxford was commissioned by the Alzheimer's Research Trust to produce a report identifying the prevalence rates for dementia and the economic cost of dementia for the UK (Luengo-Fernandez et al., 2010).

The report highlighted the following statistics.

Estimated number of people living with dementia in the UK	821,884 (this represents 1.3% of the UK population)
Approximate number of people under the age of 65 years old living with dementia in the UK	64,037 (8% of all people living with dementia in the UK)
Estimated number of women living with dementia in the UK	503,874 (61% of all people living with dementia in the UK)
Estimated number of men living with dementia in the UK	318,010 (39% of all people living with dementia in the UK)
Approximate number of people living with dementia aged 80 years or over	61%
Estimated number of people aged 65 or over living with dementia in institutionalised long-term care	304,850 (approximately 37% of all people with dementia in the UK)
Cost of dementia care to the UK economy	£23 billion per year (this is more than cancer (£12 billion per year) and heart disease (£8 billion per year) combined)
Estimated costs met by unpaid carers.	£12.4 billion (55%)
Estimated costs met by social care	£9 billion (40%)
Estimated costs met by health care	£1.2 billion (5%)

For every £1 million in care costs £129,269 is spent on cancer research, £73,153 is spent on heart disease research, £3,745 is spent on stroke research. Just £4,882 is spent on dementia research (Luengo-Fernandez et al., 2010).

ACTIVITY **1.4**

Why is it important for the information in the research summary to be explored? How could this research influence services for people with dementia? Find out how many people are living with dementia within your area and what impact this has on service funding.

It is evident that there is a need for more funding for research into dementia and also for the development of dementia-specific services.

In order to ensure that services for people with dementia are designed and delivered specifically to meet their needs it is key for health and social care services to have an understanding of dementia prevalence rates.

As identified in the report there are 64,037 people under the age of 65 years old who live with dementia. Currently services specifically aimed at this age group are very limited and therefore people living with dementia at this age often find themselves having to access services that do not meet their needs.

Views of dementia

How professionals and the wider public view dementia will have a significant impact on the experience of living with dementia. It could be argued that these views may be influenced by the history of mental illness, which stems from the 'old asylums'. The Bethlem Royal Hospital (previously known as Bedlam) is the world's first and oldest institution to specialise in mental illnesses. In the early sixteenth century the hospital was well known for its brutal treatment of patients with mental illness and would charge people to come and view the patients as a form of entertainment. This type of treatment no longer exists; however, Moore (2009) suggests that much of the negative language used to describe people with mental illness and dementia remains.

The next part of this chapter will explore the three key theoretical models that have developed over past years to try and provide alternative views of dementia: the medical model, the social model, and person-centred care.

The medical model

Innes (2002, p483) suggests that the medical model views dementia as *a progressive and irreversible disease with a prognosis of misery for the 'sufferer' and his or her family*.

The medical model is how the medical world views dementia. It continues to be the dominant approach to dementia and focuses heavily on health professionals as the experts. The model focuses on dementia as a disease and the neurological effects of dementia. Its emphasis is on the damage that is caused to the brain and the symptoms that occur.

ACTIVITY **1.5**

Describe some of the key problems with viewing dementia in this way.

> **COMMENT**
>
> *This model has been criticised for not appreciating the uniqueness of the individual's experience of dementia and for putting too much emphasis on the experience being one of constant loss. Moore (2010) states that the model has led to the development of a fabricated belief that the journey of dementia is travelled solely by the carer, while the person with dementia becomes a shell of their former self, a living shell, a living death.*

> **ACTIVITY 1.6**
>
> *What are the possible benefits of viewing dementia as a medical model?*
>
> **COMMENT**
>
> *This approach helps to develop an understanding and appreciation of the symptoms that a person may be experiencing. The medical model ensures that there continues to be research into finding a cure for dementia and the development of medical treatments such as the anti-dementia drugs.*

The social model

In the US in the early 1980s sociologists including Jaber F Gubrium and Karen A Lyman started to question the way in which the medical model viewed people with dementia. Lyman (1989) produced a paper that critiqued the medical model of dementia, arguing that the social factors that contribute to the experience are neglected. The social model does not ignore the need for the medical model but identifies that there are other factors that contribute to a person's experience of dementia, including the following.

- The influence of other people – the attitudes of other people towards dementia have a significant effect on the experience of dementia for the individual.

- Society's view of dementia – the impact of the media in portraying dementia is significant in moulding society's view.

- The environment in which the person lives – a person's surroundings can impact on the effects of the person's dementia.

Combining the two models

The introduction of multidisciplinary teams such as community mental health teams provides the opportunity to ensure that a holistic approach to supporting people with dementia is promoted. Furthermore, in a research article on GP attitudes to early diagnosis of dementia, Milne *et al.* (2005, p1) report that *fewer GP's regard early diagnosis as having negative consequences*. Additionally, they state that *those GP's who are committed regard it as an opportunity to offer preventative treatment and plan for the future . . .* (Milne *et al.*, 2005, p1). This evidence helps to ensure that at every point of a person's experience of living with dementia both the medical and the social model are considered.

Person-centred care

In addition to the work taking place in the US, psychologist Tom Kitwood developed an approach to incorporate both the social and medical models of dementia care. The term person-centred encourages health and social care professionals to focus on the person as a unique individual rather than to focus solely on the illness or disease they are experiencing. Kitwood illustrated this as:

PERSON with dementia

Vs

Person with DEMENTIA

(Kitwood, 1997, p7).

Kitwood took this principle and, following much research, developed a theory, which has underpinned the practice of dementia care – the enriched model of dementia care (Kitwood, 1997). This model identified that the medical model and the social model alone do not explain the complexity of the experience of having dementia.

The enriched model of dementia

Kitwood developed an equation to illustrate the many factors that can influence a person's experience of dementia including the neurological implications of dementia:

$$Dementia = NI+H+B+P+SP$$

NI = neurological impairment – this identifies the effects of the neurological impairment associated with dementia. While the dementia will affect a person's cognitive ability it is unlikely that a person will lose all of their abilities. Therefore we need to identify ways to enable the person with dementia to continue to utilise the skills they still retain.

H = health – this refers to the physical and mental well-being of individuals. It is an area that is often ignored in people with dementia; sometimes a deterioration in health and well-being is associated with the condition and is not investigated as a possible separate health issue.

B = biography or life history – every individual has a life history that is full of significant events and experiences. Developing knowledge of a person's past history can contribute towards achieving an understanding of a person's current behaviour.

P = personality – this relates to the individuality of people with dementia. Everybody has a unique personality and therefore the way in which people cope with the experience of dementia will be different.

SP = social psychology – how others interact and respond to people with dementia can have a significant impact on the individual's experience of dementia.

ACTIVITY *1.7*

How might this model support you in your role as a social worker?

COMMENT

Viewing dementia in this way can ensure that your approach to people with dementia is holistic and considers all elements of the person's experience, not just the disease. It ensures that you also consider the physical health needs of people with dementia and do not focus purely on the social impact of the condition.

Enriched care planning for people with dementia

Enriched care planning for people with dementia (May *et al.*, 2009) has further developed the enriched model of dementia and provides a practical framework for working with people with dementia in assessing and addressing the biological, psychological and social aspects of their lives. Its aim is to promote and maintain well-being for people with dementia and it involves five steps: profiling the person; identifying needs; documenting needs; implementing the plan; and reviewing the plan.

Psychological needs

In addition to the enriched model of dementia Kitwood also developed a concept that suggested a person's experience of dementia can be improved by focusing on what is key to all of us – our emotional and psychological needs. Kitwood argued that if these needs are unmet, *a human being cannot function, even minimally as a person* (Kitwood, 1997, p19).

The needs he identified include the following.

- Comfort – this is a person's need to experience warmth and closeness from someone or something.

- Identity – this refers to who we are as individuals. None of us is the same and we all have different identities and experiences which have shaped who we are as an individual.

- Attachment – this refers to a person's need to feel attached to the world around them and achieve a sense of security.

- Occupation – this refers to the need to be involved in the process of life, to be kept busy and occupied in a meaningful way.

- Inclusion – this refers to the need to be with others and be part of a group.

Kitwood used the image of a flower to illustrate these needs with the central need being that of love.

Personhood

Kitwood proposed that if these needs are fulfilled in a person with dementia then an individual's personhood will be maintained.

Kitwood states that personhood *is a standing or status that is bestowed upon one human being by others in the context of relationship and social being* (Kitwood 1997, p8). This is the ultimate aim of person-centred care.

Moore (2009) highlights that there are some practical issues in achieving person-centred care, including the amount of time needed to practise this type of care and the fact that carers may be blamed for a person's decline because person-centred care was not achieved. In addition, some of the terms used can be jargonistic and cause confusion.

It could also be said that person-centred care has become a term that is used to describe any form of care. To this effect other professionals have developed approaches to try and further define person-centred care and provide models of how to achieve this in practice.

VIPS

Building on the work of Kitwood, the VIPS model identifies that the key elements of person-centred care (PCC) involve maintaining the value base of personhood, providing individualised assessment and care, taking the perspective of the person with dementia and providing a supportive social psychology (Brooker, 2007). Brooker (2007) illustrates this through the following equation:

$$PCC = V + I + P + S$$

where

V = values people with dementia

I = treats people as individuals

P = perspective of person with dementia

S = supportive social psychology.

Brooker and Surr (2005) highlight that no one part of the equation is more directional than the other, they are all contributory, and draw attention to the acronym's other meaning of very important persons.

Feelings matter most

In his recent book *Achieving real outcomes in dementia care homes* Sheard (2011) identifies the approach of Dementia Care Matters as:

> *'Person centred care is about the belief in life that 'Feelings Matter Most'.*
>
> *Person centred care is an approach to life.*
>
> *It is something we 'feel' and 'are' not something to just 'do'.*
>
> *In a care home this is why feelings based care is so important.*
>
> *Staff need to have heart and a desire to connect and reach people.*

Sheard goes on to state that Dementia Care Matters' additional definition of person cen-tred care for 2011 is:

Person

Experiences

Reality differently

Searching for

Our empathy and

Nurturing

Malignant social psychology

During his time researching and working with people with dementia Kitwood further iden-tified that *if we come close to the details of how life is lived, hour by hour and minute by minute, we can see many processes that contribute towards the undermining of people with dementia* (Kitwood, 1997, p45). He termed this *malignant social psychology* and out-lined ten types of approach that can have a negative and damaging effect for a person with dementia. The list was extended to 17 through the work of the University of Bradford and the development of Dementia Care Mapping, which will be discussed later in this chapter. The list is as follows.

Intimidation	Disempowerment
Withholding	Imposition
Outpacing	Disruption
Infantilisation	Objectification
Labelling	Stigmatisation
Disparagement	Ignoring
Accusation	Banishment
Treachery	Mockery
Invalidation	

ACTIVITY *1.8*

Why might malignant social psychology occur within a dementia care setting?

COMMENT

While the word malignant signifies something very harmful and symptomatic of a care environment that is deeply damaging to personhood, possibly even undermining physical well-being, it does not imply evil intent on the part of the caregivers; most of their work is done with kindness and good intent. The malignancy is part of our cultural inheritance (Kitwood, 1997). Brooker and Surr (2005) highlight that malignant social psychology has become 'unchallenged and interwoven' in the care culture and spreads from one staff member to another very quickly.

CASE STUDY

John was diagnosed with Alzheimer's disease approximately three years ago. He lives at home with his wife, Pauline. For the past couple of months John has been receiving personal care support from a domiciliary care agency as Pauline was starting to find it hard to care for John 24 hours a day. Pauline has noticed that the care staff talk about John in front of him and she has overheard them telling him that 'You just said that' and more recently has observed the care staff taking John's flannel from him and commenting that it will be quicker if they do the job themselves. Over a period of time John has started to do less and less for himself and has become quieter and more withdrawn.

Positive person work

In response to malignant social psychology Kitwood (1997) identified interactions that could promote and maintain an individual's personhood. He termed this *positive person work*. He identified a number of positive interactions that could increase well-being in a person with dementia and ensure that their personhood was upheld. These are listed below.

Warmth	Holding
Relaxed pace	Respect
Acceptance	Facilitation
Collaboration	Recognition
Celebration	Acknowledgement
Genuineness	Validation
Empowerment	Enabling
Including	Belonging

Observing the lived experience

In order to fully appreciate the experience of dementia and the potentially damaging effects of malignant social psychology and the significant impact of positive person work, Kitwood developed a process called Dementia Care Mapping (DCM). He described this as *a serious attempt to take the standpoint of the person with dementia, using a combination of empathy and observational skill* (Kitwood, 1997, p.4).

Through the work of the University of Bradford DCM has been further developed and is now used as an observational tool in dementia settings such as hospital wards, care homes and day services, with many people trained in the use of the tool. Brooker and Surr (2005) describe DCM as *both a tool and a process. The tool is the observations and the coding frames. This is the intensive in-depth, real time observations over a number of hours of people with dementia living in formal care settings. The process, is the use of DCM as a driver for the development of person-centred care practice* . . .

In addition Dean *et al.* (1993) developed the quality of interactions schedule (QUIS) to aid in evaluating the perspective of people living within two residential domus units for older people with mental illness. Sheard (2008) has developed this tool further to assist with measuring quality of life for people with dementia living within a residential setting. Sheard states that *the aim of an observation is for the observer to become the eyes, ears, heart and voice of people with a dementia* (Sheard, 2008, p14).

CHAPTER SUMMARY

This chapter has introduced you to the term dementia and highlighted common groups of dementia and their associated symptoms while also considering the term person-centred care.

The first section of the chapter examined the differences in the most common groups of dementia and considered the signs and symptoms that a person with dementia may experience. Furthermore it considered the experience of living with dementia and the possible impact this has on the lives of the person living with dementia and their carer.

The second section of the chapter identified two of the different types of medicines that are prescribed to people with dementia and considered the NICE guidance surrounding the availability of the anti-dementia drugs and also the negative effects of the use of antipsychotic drugs.

The chapter went on to compare the different theoretical models of dementia including the medical and social model and furthermore reflected upon the influence of Tom Kitwood in defining person-centred care. In addition the chapter identified the other professionals who have developed the work of Tom Kitwood and looked at the VIPS model and the Feelings Matter Most approach.

Finally the chapter examined the effects of malignant social psychology as defined by Tom Kitwood and examined the use of tools that try to observe the lived experience of dementia for people in care settings.

This will continue to be an area that will develop over the next few years as we strive to improve the lives of people with dementia. Your role as a social worker will be integral in trying to achieve this.

The next chapter will explore the role of social work in supporting people with dementia and their carers. It will further consider recent government policies, strategies and legislation and will examine the role social work has in implementing and interpreting these.

Brooker, D (2006) *Person-centred dementia care: Making services better*. London: Jessica Kingsley Publishers.

This book gives fresh definition to the important ideas behind and the implementation of person-centred care for people with dementia and explains four key elements of person-centred care that comprises the VIPS model.

Bryden, C (2005) *Dancing with dementia: My story of living positively with dementia*. London: Jessica Kingsley Publishers.

This book is a vivid account of the author's experience of living with dementia, exploring the effects of memory problems, loss of independence, difficulties in communication and the exhaustion of coping with simple tasks.

Goldsmith, M (2002) *Hearing the voice of people with dementia: Opportunities and obstacles*. London: Jessica Kingsley Publishers.

This book explores the idea that communication is not only possible, but also vital to the understanding and the development of services.

Kitwood, T (1997) *Dementia reconsidered: The person comes first*.

This groundbreaking book critically scrutinises and reappraises the older ideas of dementia. The unifying theme is the personhood of men and women who have dementia – an issue that was neglected for many years in both psychiatry and care practice.

May, H, Edwards, P and Brooker, B (2009) *Enriched care planning for people with dementia: A good practice guide to delivering person-centred care*. London: Jessica Kingsley Publishers.

This book presents a complete practical framework for whole-person assessment, care planning and review of persons with dementia or signs of dementia who are in need of, or already receiving, health and/or social support.

Moore, D (2010) *Explaining Alzheimer's and dementia – more than memories*. Brighton: Emerald Publishing.

This book provides an accessible, easy-to-read introduction to the experience of Alzheimer's disease and discusses different behaviours and forms of communication.

Sheard, D (2007) *Being: An approach to life and dementia*. London: Alzheimer's Society and Dementia Care Matters.

This publication is the first of five books in the innovative 'Feelings Matter Most' series. *Being* promotes a new approach to what it takes to be person-centred. The book introduces the idea that feelings matter most in dementia care.

Stokes, G (2010) *And still the music plays – stories of people with dementia*. London: Hawker Publications.

In this book Stokes draws on his memories of people with dementia whom he has met, in order to bring us all a greater understanding of the condition and of why some people behave in the way they do.

www.alzheimerssociety.org.uk

This website is fundamental in developing knowledge regarding dementia and provides many factsheets on the different types of dementia.

www.scie.gov.uk

This website includes an e-learning programme which is aimed at anyone who comes into contact with someone with dementia and provides a general introduction to the disease and the experience of living with dementia.

www.mentalhealth.org.uk

The Mental Health Foundation website contains various publications including a booklet aimed at providing an explanation of how people with dementia might feel and behave to young people.

Chapter 2

Legislation, guidance and dementia

Introduction

When working in social work with older adults it is important that you are aware of legislation, guidance and policies relating to the field of dementia care, because it is this knowledge that allows you to: *unpick legislative guidance and maximise independence and opportunities for service users and their carers* (Burrow, 2009, p74). Furthermore, this accords with the British Association of Social Workers' *Code of Ethics* (2002).

Possibly more than any other service user group people living with dementia have faced a history of discrimination and denial of their autonomy. This discrimination has been demonstrated in numerous documents including research (Chan and Chan, 2009, p221) and reports such as the Alzheimer's Society's *Is free nursing care unfair and unworkable?* (2002), Carruthers and Ormondroyd's document *Age equality in health and social care* (2009) and the Scottish Government's *Standards of care for dementia in Scotland: Action to support the change programme* (Mental Welfare Commission for Scotland, 2011, p3).

Hence your role to understand legislation and use it to *maximise independence and opportunities* and promote autonomy will be even more important with this group of individuals and their families.

This chapter will explore different pieces of legislation and guidance with particular focus on:

- the National Dementia Strategy (2009);

- the Department of Health's guidance on risk for people with dementia, *Nothing ventured, nothing gained* (2010c);

- the Mental Capacity Act 2005; and

- the Human Rights Act 1998.

This chapter will help readers to:

- consider why a National Dementia Strategy was/is needed;

- reflect on the role of social worker in relation to specific objectives of the strategy;

- be aware of the issues faced with the implementation of the strategy;

- consider how taking a measured risk can be beneficial to the well-being of people with dementia;

- contemplate the importance of a balanced approach to risk;

- examine the different elements of the Mental Capacity Act 2005 and the Human Rights Act (1998);

- be aware of other relevant pieces of legislation and guidance.

The National Dementia Strategy (2009)

The National Dementia Strategy for England was launched by the Department of Health in 2009. A strategy has also been published in Northern Ireland and Scotland. In Wales dementia action plans have been published. For the purpose of this chapter the emphasis will be on England's strategy, the rationale for this being the fact that it was the first of the UK strategies to be launched. However, there is information about each country's strategy at the end of the chapter.

ACTIVITY **2.1**

Write three reasons why you think a National Dementia Strategy was needed.

COMMENT

Some of the reasons why a strategy was needed were in order to:

- *plan how to support the growing number of people with dementia. As Chapter 1 highlighted, the number of people with dementia in the UK is increasing. The current estimate of 750,000 people with dementia in the UK is expected to increase to 940,000 people by 2021 and 1.7 million people by 2051 (Alzheimer's Society, 2007a).Other research suggests that this figure may be even higher with current estimates being closer to 820,000 people with dementia (Luengo-Fernandez et al., 2010, p3).*

Continued

- *improve health and social care services for people with dementia and their families. A number of reports have highlighted the inadequate support people with dementia receive in hospitals (Alzheimer's Society, 2009; Royal College of Psychiatrists, 2011) and care homes (Laing and Buisson, 2009; Alzheimer's Society, 2007b);*

- *manage the significant financial challenge dementia poses the UK economy. It is estimated that dementia currently costs the UK economy £17 billion every year. This figure is expected to rise to over £50 billion every year within 30 years' time (Alzheimer's Society, 2007a). Other figures predict an annual increase from £15 billion in 2008 to £23 billion in 2018 if improvements are not made to the cost-effectiveness of services (King's Fund, 2008). However, other estimates suggest that the economic impact of dementia is already costing the UK £23 billion with an annual cost of £9 billion for social care alone (Luengo-Fernandez et al., 2010, p11).*

The 17 objectives

To try and meet these challenges the strategy outlined 17 objectives, listed below.

1. Improving public and professional awareness and understanding of dementia.

2. Good-quality early diagnosis and intervention for all.

3. Good-quality information for those with diagnosed dementia and their carers.

4. Enabling easy access to care, support and advice following diagnosis.

5. Development of structured peer support and learning networks.

6. Improved community personal support services.

7. Implementing the Carers' Strategy.

8. Improved quality of care for people with dementia in general hospitals.

9. Improved intermediate care for people with dementia.

10. Considering the potential for housing support, housing-related services and telecare to support people with dementia and their carers.

11. Living well with dementia in care homes.

12. Improved end-of-life care for people with dementia.

13. An informed and effective workforce for people with dementia.

14. A joint commissioning strategy for dementia.

15. Improved assessment and regulation of health and care services and of how systems are working for people with dementia and their carers.

16. A clear picture of research evidence and needs.

17. Effective national and regional support for implementation of the Strategy.

ACTIVITY *2.2*

In your opinion which of the 17 objectives are particularly relevant to the role of social work?

COMMENT

It could certainly be argued that social work has a role to play in all of the objectives. However, there are a number of particularly relevant objectives including objectives 1, 3, 4, 6 and 11. These will now be looked at in more detail.

Objective 1: Improving public and professional awareness and understanding of dementia. Although it may be seen that this is mainly the role of health professionals it is essential that social workers are involved in this promotion to balance the medical model view of dementia with a social disability model (see Chapter 1). Social workers are in a pivotal position to raise awareness about anti-discriminatory practice and to promote the rights of people living with dementia. However, there is also a significant need to raise the understanding of dementia among social workers. Research by Moore and Jones (2011) indicated that there are still assumptions made by social workers relating to the abilities of people with dementia.

Objective 3: Good-quality information for those with diagnosed dementia and their carers. This is another significant role for social workers, who may be the first port of call for individuals or an ongoing source of information. Consequently, as a social worker you need to be able either to provide information yourself or signpost individuals on to other services, such as the Alzheimer's Society, Admiral nurses or advocacy services. As NICE–SCIE guidance on supporting people with dementia and their carers in health and social care states: *social care professionals should inform people with dementia and their carers about advocacy services and voluntary support, and should encourage their use* (NICE–SCIE, 2007, p15).

ACTIVITY *2.3*

What are advocacy services? Why can they be so helpful for people with dementia? Find out what advocacy services are available for people with dementia in your area.

COMMENT

Advocacy, in the simplest of terms, describes a situation when someone speaks up for or acts on the behalf of another. An advocacy service can help a person with dementia to make their views or wishes known to others. This is so important because some people with dementia may have difficulty in verbally communicating their point of view, resulting in their wishes being ignored by others.

Objective 4: Enabling easy access to care, support and advice following diagnosis. The role of social workers in implementing the fourth objective is also relevant as the provision of care, support and advice is fundamental to social work. The importance of this was highlighted by a study by Brodaty *et al.* (2005) which found that people with dementia and their families were more likely to access services provided by health, social care and charities if they had support from a social worker.

Objective 6: Improved community personal support services. This objective has particular relevance due to its emphasis on community support. The strategy states the need for people with dementia to have: *Access to flexible and reliable services, ranging from early intervention to specialist home care services, which are responsive to the personal needs and preferences of each individual and take account of their broader family circumstances* (DoH 2009a, p46).

The above stresses the need for services including the following.

* *Early intervention services.* Often people with dementia may come into contact with social services at a time of crisis. For example, a family member can no longer care for a person with dementia and social services is contacted for help. However, there is a growing argument about the role social workers can have with early intervention and preventative services such as re-enablement or telecare services (see Chapter 5). Access to these services will depend on varying factors including availability within a locality and if there are eligibility criteria for a service.

* *Home care services.* The strategy's emphasis on this is understandable considering that two-thirds of people with dementia live in their own home or in a family member's home. Furthermore the evidence suggests that the majority of people with dementia want to stay in their own home for as long as possible (Alzheimer's Society, 2010e).

Currently care at home (domiciliary care) provided by or commissioned by councils accounts for a large proportion of annual adult social care costs. It is probable that this will increase in accordance with the increasing prevalence of people with dementia. In 2008/9 £1 out of every £4 spent by local authorities on adult social care was spent on home care and 75 per cent of individuals who received this care were over the age of 65 (Care Quality Commission, 2010).

Despite this level of spending a number of reports have highlighted the inadequacies of home care services, including limited visiting times (for example, 15 minutes) and the lack of consistency among home care workers (Alzheimer's Society, 2011c; the Care Council for Wales, 2010; Commission for Social Care Inspection (CSCI), 2006). These issues may be particularly difficult for people with dementia as familiarity with staff and being given the time to feel supported are crucial to their feelings of well-being. Further evidence indicates that specialist home care support for people with dementia can be both beneficial to a person with dementia and cost-effective as it reduces unnecessary and early admission into care homes (Rothera *et al.*, 2007; Gaugler *et al.*, 2005, p177). It is estimated that placement in care homes currently costs £7 billion a year with two-thirds of this being paid for by local authorities (Knapp *et al.*, 2007).

Therefore, along with your colleagues and commissioners of services, you will need to consider the cost-effectiveness of a service and whether or not it is *responsive to the personal needs and preferences of each individual.* This, now more than ever, is important with the current government's emphasis on reduction of spending and greater local and individual control.

RESEARCH SUMMARY

In January 2011 the Alzheimer's Society published a study relating to care at home for people with dementia, Support, Stay, Save. The report collected evidence across England, Wales and Northern Ireland from over 2,000 people with dementia, their carers and home care workers. The study found the following:

- *83 per cent of people with dementia and their carers said that remaining in their own home was very important to them.*

- *59 per cent of people with dementia and their carers said being active in their local community was very important.*

- *50 per cent of people with dementia and their carers felt that they were not receiving sufficient care to meet their needs.*

- *52 per cent of carers felt that were not getting sufficient support to enable them to care for the person with dementia. Caring for someone can lead to numerous repercussions for a person's mental and physical health and it seems that the feeling that not enough support is being given exacerbates these problems.*

- *37 per cent of carers questioned had been made aware of their right to a carers' assessment.*

ACTIVITY **2.4**

The report by the Alzheimer's Society demonstrated a number of issues relating to care of people with dementia at home. One issue was the number of carers who were not made aware of their legal right to ask for a separate carers' assessment (the Carers (Equal Opportunities) Act 2004).

Consider why it is so important for carers of people with dementia to be made aware of this right.

COMMENT

Being made aware of this right to ask for a carers' assessment provides carers with the opportunity to discuss the support they may be entitled to. Such support can reduce levels of stress for family members, reduce difficult behaviours in people with dementia, maintain a positive relationship between the carer and the person with dementia and enable family carers to continue caring for a person with dementia for longer (Moniz-Cook et al., 2008, p188; Zarit, S et al., 1980, p652). Furthermore, undertaking the assessment is an opportunity to identify any difficulties the carer is experiencing. As guidance from NICE states: Those carrying out carers' assessment should seek to identify any psychological distress and the psychosocial impact on the carer (NICE–SCIE, 2007, p36).

Objective 11: Living well with dementia in care homes. Social work is a crucial part of making this objective reality due to the multifaceted relationship a social worker can have with a person with dementia, their family and the care home.

ACTIVITY 2.5

Suggest three different ways in which social workers can support care home staff and managers to enable people with dementia to live well in care homes.

COMMENT

There are numerous ways that a social worker can help. Some examples are given below.

- *Social workers can provide advice to staff in care homes. It is clear that many staff in care homes do not receive adequate training on how to support people with dementia and their families (Laing and Buisson, 2009) and although social workers cannot provide this training they can certainly be a source of advice to staff by suggesting different ways of supporting people with dementia.*

- *They can highlight different psychosocial interventions. Psychosocial interventions focus on supporting an individual's psychological needs and their interactions with their social environment. They include cognitive stimulation therapy (Aguirre et al., 2010) and therapies such as snoezelen (Baker et al., 2003).*

- *They can suggest ways of meaningfully occupying people with dementia, including creative therapies (Allan and Killick 2000; Coaten, 2001), reminiscence and life-story work (Woods et al., 2009). Research by the Alzheimer's Society (2007b) has highlighted the limited opportunities for activity that many people with dementia have in care homes.*

We have now considered a number of the different objectives of the strategy and explored the possible role that social workers have to play in each of these. Next we will focus on some of the challenges faced in the implementation of the strategy.

Challenges to implementation

There can be no doubt that the publication of the National Dementia Strategy was a very important step forward in meeting some of the problems mentioned earlier in this chapter. However, a number of recent reports have indicated the challenges that localities face in the implementation of the strategy including:

- problems with leadership in moving the strategy forward (National Audit Office, 2010);

- lack of clarity about spending of extra funding. Primary care trusts (PCTs) in England had received funding of £150 million to support the strategy within the first two years (National Audit Office, 2010);

- limited joint planning. A report by the All-Party Parliamentary Group on Dementia (2010) found that half of PCTs and local authority partnerships had not met the March 2010 deadline for a joint implementation plan.

Possibly as a result of such issues or as a consequence of a change in government a revised implementation plan was launched. This prioritised four of the original 17 objectives. These are:

- good-quality early diagnosis and intervention for all;

- improved quality of care in general hospitals;

- living well with dementia in care homes; and

- reduced use of antipsychotic medication.

Although the emphasis of the objectives does seem to be health care, the implementation plan emphasises that: *the improvement of community personal support services is integral to and underpins each of the four priorities as it supports early intervention, prevents premature admission to care homes and impacts on inappropriate admission to hospital and length of stay* (DoH, 2010b, p10).

Hence the role of social workers and community support is still an essential ingredient in the implementation of the strategy.

Nothing ventured, nothing gained (2010)

As an accompaniment to the revised implementation plan the Department of Health launched a guide on risk and people with dementia. This document aims to *help people with dementia, family carers, and practitioners negotiate a shared approach to positive risk taking* (DoH, 2010c, p8).

ACTIVITY 2.6

Consider how taking measured risks can be positive for a person with dementia.

COMMENT

You may have suggested a number of positives for a person. The following quote from a person with dementia highlights some of the possible benefits.

Each day brings its own catalogue of risks, some minor and some dangerous. But over time and with forgetting, there is the risk of being put on the sidelines, of being seen as a hindrance, and having control taken away from you, under the guise of it being for your own good. So, while we can, we must challenge the risks . . . People living with a dementia must be allowed to take risks, because if we don't, we are in danger of relaxing into the disease. At times we feel hopeless. At times the hurt we feel is indescribable and we can let it be a barrier to life. But there is a life for us, if we risk it.

(Morgan, 2009, p28)

In the past a safety first approach to risk was frequently adopted in social work (Titterton, 2005). Although this approach often reduced the risk to a person's physical health, in many instances it was undertaken to the detriment of psychosocial needs. Consequently the Department of Health guidance is based on *balancing the positive benefits of taking risks against the risks of an adverse event occurring* (DoH, 2010c, p8). How this can be achieved is highlighted in the following case study.

CASE STUDY

William is 54 and is in the early stages of dementia; he lives with his wife in their own home. He has always been a keen walker and has continued to enjoy walking for a number of miles each day, despite his dementia. Recently William confided to his social worker, Mark, that he is starting to have trouble finding his way home and is thinking about stopping this activity. Together they discussed both the positives and negatives of William's daily walks and in the end felt that the benefits outweighed the negative effects. They also discussed a number of strategies to help William feel at ease about continuing his walking and to reduce the risk of his becoming lost. They considered the possibility of using assistive technology or finding another person who would be keen to walk with William.

The case study highlights how social workers can work with individuals to balance the positives and negatives relating to risk. In the case of William the risk of getting lost needs to be set against the risks of William losing his independence, becoming bored, no longer socialising with others he meets while walking, his wife not having respite from caring while William is walking, and so on. It also shows the role of social workers in giving advice about different strategies to reduce risk.

Having examined the National Dementia Strategy and the *Nothing ventured, nothing gained* risk guidance, we shall go on to concentrate on some of the legislation that is relevant to people with dementia. We shall start by discussing the Mental Capacity Act 2005.

The Mental Capacity Act 2005

The Mental Capacity Act (MCA) 2005 came into force in 2007. The main purpose of the Act is to set out what should happen when an adult is unable (lacks the capacity) to make specific decisions at a particular time for themselves. As was discussed in Chapter 1, dementia can affect the cognitive abilities associated with decision making, which can result in a person lacking the capacity to make certain decisions. However, this does not necessarily mean that a person lacks capacity to make any decisions at all. For example, a person in the later experience of dementia may not have the ability to make major decisions, such as whether or not to sell their house, but they still may be able to make decisions about what time they get up in the morning, what they have to eat and so on.

ACTIVITY **2.7**

How do you know if a person has the capacity to make certain decisions?

COMMENT

You may have found it difficult to answer this, and until the introduction of the MCA 2005 this was a challenge many practitioners faced. However, the MCA 2005 has made this easier by providing a two-stage test of capacity.

Test of capacity

The first part of the test asks us to consider if *the person has an impairment of the mind or brain, or is there some other sort of disturbance affecting the way their mind works?*

In the case of a person with dementia, if we concentrated purely on the first part of this test, we would presume that the person lacked capacity because they have an *impairment of the brain*. This assumption, conjoined with the challenges of communication that many people with dementia can face, has led to the right of people with dementia to be involved in decision making being ignored or dismissed.

To prevent this happening, it is essential that you consider the second part of the test. This emphasises the need to consider if *the impairment or disturbance means that the person is unable to make the decision in question at the time it needs to be made.*

This second part of the test recognises the need for an assessment of a capacity to be decision- and time-specific. This is particularly relevant to people with dementia where, due to the fluctuating effects of dementia, a person's ability to make a decision can vary. This is highlighted in the following case study.

CASE STUDY

Margaret is an 87-year-old woman who has dementia with Lewy bodies. She lives with her husband in their own home. Margaret currently receives support from a home care agency twice a week; however, the agency is shortly closing down. Her social worker, Sally, went to visit Margaret and her husband to explain the situation to her. Sally wanted to assess Margaret's ability to make the decision about using a different home care provider. However, Margaret seemed unresponsive to Sally's questions. Margaret's husband explained that she had been awake for most of the night. Sally agreed to visit again later in the week. When Sally returned Margaret was more responsive and seemed to understand and retain the information. Sally assessed that with the right support Margaret has the capacity to make the decision about a new provider of care.

ACTIVITY 2.8

Consider the case of Margaret above. How do you think Sally came to the conclusion that Margaret has the capacity to make a decision about the change in home care provider?

COMMENT

The case study shows that when Sally assessed Margaret's capacity she considered both parts of the test of capacity. She understood that in assessing Margaret's capacity she needed to be both time- and decision-specific. Margaret was not able to make the decision during Sally's first visit but with the appropriate support was able to on the second visit. Sally would have assessed that Margaret lacked the capacity to make this decision if she was unable to do one or more of the following:

1. *understand the information relevant to the decision;*

2. *retain that information;*

3. *use or weigh that information as part of the process of making the decision; or*

4. *communicate the decision (whether by talking, using sign language or other means) (MCA 2005, p2).*

Five principles

To provide further guidance the MCA 2005 is governed by five principles. The case study of Rose will be used to clarify these principles.

CASE STUDY

Rose is an 85-year-old woman with dementia who has been on a hospital ward for the past three months. Originally she was admitted after a serious fall at home, where she lives by herself; however other complications have led to a longer stay. During this time her only visitor has been her sister. Rose has trouble with speech and writing and she is described by the ward staff as disruptive, particularly at meal times and visiting hours. It is felt that it would be in her best interests to move into a care home. Ian, the hospital social worker, has come to visit Rose to assess her capacity to make the decision to move into a care home.

Principle 1: A person must be assumed to have capacity unless it is established that he/she lacks capacity. This means that people without dementia cannot decide that a person with dementia lacks capacity, or make assumptions about what is best for a person, simply on the basis of a person having dementia. This is such a significant principle because it challenges stereotypical presumptions that all people with dementia are unable to make decisions because of their condition. In the case study nobody could make the assumption that Rose was unable to make a decision about moving into a care home based simply on the fact that she has dementia.

Principle 2: A person is not to be treated as unable to make a decision unless all practicable steps to help him/her to do so have been taken without success. This means that those involved in the support of a person with dementia should make sure that all the necessary support needed to make a decision is presented to the person with dementia in a way that they will understand. In the example of Rose, the social worker should take the necessary steps to make sure that Rose receives the support needed. For example it would be important to make sure that Rose is in an appropriate environment. Being on a noisy hospital ward may influence Rose's ability to make a decision, whereas discussing the options in a quiet side room may be more helpful. Similarly, because Rose has difficulty with speech, other forms of communication would need to be considered, as well as different tools to impart the information, such as talking mats (Macer, 2011, p37). Furthermore, owing to the reason for Rose's admission to hospital, it would be important to consider if she was in pain and if this was influencing her ability to make a decision. The evidence indicates that pain management in people with dementia is poor (Scherder, 2000, p6).

Principle 3. A person is not to be treated as unable to make a decision merely because he/she makes an unwise decision. This means that those without dementia cannot presume that a person with dementia lacks capacity just because they have done something that seems unwise. In the example of Rose, if she were assessed as having capacity and decided to return to her own home this may be viewed as an unwise decision because of the risk to her safety, since she might fall again. However, we must not presume that Rose lacks capacity to make this decision merely on the basis that it seems unwise to Ian or others involved in her care.

Principle 4: An act done, or decision made, under this Act for or on behalf of a person who lacks capacity must be done, or made, in his/her best interests.

ACTIVITY **2.9**

Consider what the term best interests *means and reflect upon how you can make sure you are acting in a person's best interests.*

COMMENT

The term best interests *means that when you make a decision for a person who lacks capacity, you have to make sure that it is the best one for them. However, deciding what is in the person's best interests is not always a straightforward task, so there is a Code of Practice to aid in this. As practitioners, social workers involved in making decisions on behalf of a person with dementia who lacks capacity are* legally required to have regard to relevant guidance in the Code of Practice and should be able to explain how they have had regard to the Code when acting or making decisions *(Department for Constitutional Affairs, 2007, p2). In other words you will need to be aware of the Code of Practice and demonstrate how you have followed the Code when making decisions on behalf of a person with dementia who lacks capacity.*

In the example of Rose, the Code of Practice for the MCA 2005 could assist if it was assessed that she did not have the capacity to make the decision to move into the care home. The Code asks us to consider the following points.

Continued

COMMENT *continued*

- If there is a possibility that the person will regain capacity, can the decision be delayed until then? *In Rose's case it is possible that the other complications she experienced in hospital may be affecting her ability to make a decision about moving into the care home. Leaving this to a later date, when she has recovered from these complications, may mean that Rose is more able to make this decision.*

- The person's past and present wishes, beliefs and values should be taken into account and the views of those who are close to them should also be considered. *In Rose's case it is possible that she had previously declared her wish not to move into a care home. This would need to be considered. Rose's sister's opinion should also be taken into account.*

- The process used to arrive at the person's best interest should be carefully recorded and reviewed regularly as what is in the person's best interest may change over time. *With Rose it may be in her best interests to move into a care home at the moment. However, it may be found that what is in Rose's best interests now changes and an alternative form of support should be sought.*

Principle 5: Before the act is done, or the decision is made, regard must be had to whether the purpose for which it is needed can be as effectively achieved in a way that is less restrictive of the person's rights and freedom of action. The individual who makes a decision for the person who lacks capacity must consider how to make this decision in a way that infringes as little as possible on a person's rights. In the case of Rose, if she lacked capacity, a decision would have to be made in a way that is least restrictive to her rights and freedom. For instance it may be felt that moving to a care home may be less restrictive of Rose's freedom compared to the hospital ward.

Other elements of the MCA 2005

There are many other elements of the MCA 2005 and some of these will now be looked at briefly. Further reading should be sought for a more detailed explanation.

Some of these elements include the following.

- Advanced care planning. This term covers a number of processes that enable people who currently have capacity to have the opportunity to make preparations for a time when they may lack capacity. For instance a person in the early experience of dementia may be able to make an advanced decision about certain types of future treatment they receive under the MCA 2005. However, as Clare (2004, p180) warns, even in the early stages of dementia a person's cognitive ability will be impaired and so the process is not straightforward.

NICE guidance states that:

> Health and social care professionals should discuss with the person with dementia, while he or she still has capacity, and his or her carer the use of:

- *advance statements (which allow people to state what is to be done if they should subsequently lose the capacity to decide or to communicate)*

- *advance decisions to refuse treatment*

- *Lasting Power of Attorney (a legal document that allows people to state in writing who they want to make certain decisions for them if they cannot make them for themselves, including decisions about personal health and welfare)*

- *a Preferred Place of Care Plan (which allows people to record decisions about future care choices and the place where the person would like to die).*

(NICE–SCIE, 2007, p16)

- Independent Mental Capacity advocate (IMCA). An IMCA can support a person with dementia who lacks capacity to make specific decisions and does not have anyone, such as friends or family, to 'speak' for them. These specific decisions include decisions being made about a person's accommodation, reviews of accommodation and serious medical treatment. In such situations local authorities and NHS bodies have a duty to appoint an IMCA.

- The Court of Protection. This court can appoint decision makers, known as deputies, for a person who lacks capacity. Furthermore if a person with dementia disagrees with a finding that they lack capacity they can take this to the Court of Protection for review.

- Deprivation of Liberty Safeguards (DOLS). In 2009 the Mental Capacity Act was amended to include the Deprivation of Liberty Safeguards. This key addition made it unlawful to deprive an individual, who lacks capacity and has not been compulsorily detained under the Mental Health Act 2007, of their liberty without a number of safeguards being followed and only if a less restrictive alternative is not available (Ministry of Justice, 2008). The aim of these safeguards is to prevent an individual having their liberty taken away by a hospital or care home without authorisation from a supervisory body (in the case of care homes this body would be the local authority), which has to comply with a number of safeguards.

ACTIVITY 2.10

The Deprivation of Liberty Safeguards apply only to care home and hospital settings. Evaluate the implications this may have for social workers who believe a family member is depriving a person of their liberty in their own home.

COMMENT

You may have considered a number of implications. As a social worker you may have to work with family members to find out why the person with dementia is being deprived of their liberty. For example, is it because the family member is not aware of services that may help, or because they believe there are no alternatives? You would need to work with families to consider alternatives. However, safeguarding procedures need to be followed (see Chapter 3).

Despite the positive steps the MCA 2005 has made, others have argued that it does not go far enough to protect the rights of people with dementia (Stewart, 2006, p118; Boyle, 2008). Hence it is so important that in your practice you are aware of both the MCA 2005 and the Human Rights Act 1998.

The Human Rights Act 1998

The Human Rights Act 1998 came into effect in the UK in 2000. There are a number of rights, which are referred to as articles. Some of the rights are absolute rights such as Articles 2 and 3. This means that these rights are fundamental and should never be constrained. Some of the other articles are known as limited rights, such as Article 5. For instance, a person's right to liberty can be limited if an individual is detained under the Mental Health Act 2007.

Below is a list of some of the human rights. These include:

- Article 2: The right to life;

- Article 3: The right to freedom from torture and degrading treatment;

- Article 5: The right to liberty;

- Article 8: The right to respect for private and family life;

- Article 9: The right to freedom of thought, conscience and religion;

- Article 10: The right to freedom of expression;

- Article 14: The right not to be discriminated against in respect of these rights and freedoms.

Although these rights apply to everyone in the UK, people with dementia may be at an increased risk of having these rights violated.

ACTIVITY 2.11

Suggest three reasons why people with dementia are particularly vulnerable to having their human rights breached.

COMMENT

There are a number of possibilities you may have suggested including the following.

- *A person with dementia may find it difficult to report a violation of their human rights due to communication difficulties.*

- *A person with dementia may not be believed by others.*

- *A person may not be aware of what human rights they have.*

- *A person may not know that their human rights are being breached and so do not make others aware.*

These reasons indicate why it is important in your role as a social worker for you to be aware of this legislation, so that you can recognise and uphold these rights.

What is a public authority

Another reason why people with dementia may be at a greater risk of having their human rights breached is because of the current ambiguity around the term public authority. This term relates to all central and local government agencies, including social services and any organisation *whose functions are of a public nature*, and such organisations have a duty to respect and uphold individuals' human rights. However, this definition has been broadly interpreted, with the result that not all care homes run by private companies are treated as public authorities, as demonstrated in the following case.

The case of Mrs YL (2007)

Mrs YL was an older adult with dementia. Birmingham City Council had a statutory duty to make arrangements for her care and accommodation under the National Assistance Act (1948). Consequently Mrs YL moved into a care home run by a private company. The company wanted to remove Mrs YL from the home and served her daughter with 28 days' notice of this. Legal proceedings were launched on the grounds that moving Mrs YL from the care home would breach a number of her human rights. However, the House of Lords decided that a private care home providing care and accommodation for an older adult under contract with a local authority was not exercising functions of a public nature and was therefore not a public authority. This meant that the claim that Mrs YL's rights were being violated was rejected.

ACTIVITY **2.12**

Regarding the above case discuss with a colleague what some of the implications may be of such a ruling for other people living in a privately run care home.

COMMENT

This ruling seems to place people living in privately run care homes in an unfair position compared to those living in a home run by a local authority. However, this anomaly was addressed in section 145 of the Health and Social Care Act 2008. Changes were made that enable a person who is placed in a private care home by a local authority to be covered by human rights legislation. Nevertheless this ambiguity still remains when it comes to individuals who privately fund their place in a care home and with individuals who receive care in their own home by a private company or who employ a personal assistant through their personal budget. Despite a number of calls for this discrepancy to be eliminated (Equality and Human Rights Commission, 2011) it remains. Therefore it is even more essential to stress your professional duty to safeguard vulnerable adults living in their own homes. These people are at an even greater risk of experiencing abuse because, unlike other individuals, they may not have the legislative protection of the Human Rights Act 1998. The subject of safeguarding adults and its relation to the Human Rights Act 1998 will be discussed further in Chapter 3.

Other legislation/strategies

There are numerous other pieces of legislation and strategies that are relevant to people with dementia due to the nature and numbers of people affected by dementia. Not all are listed here but they include the following.

- The Carers' Strategy (2008). This strategy (carers at the heart of twenty-first-century families and communities) sets out plans to improve support for carers (including carers of people with dementia) over a ten-year period. In 2010 the government launched a document, *Recognised, valued and supported: Next steps for the carers' strategy* (DoH, 2010d). This prioritised a number of areas relating to the strategy over a four-year period.

- The National End of Life Care Strategy (2008). This strategy covered 12 key areas to try to improve end of life care for all adults, including people with dementia.

- The Equality Act (2010). The Act aims to protect people from discrimination because of age, disability, gender, race, sexual orientation, religion or belief.

- *Everybody's business. Integrated mental health services for older adults: a service development guide* (Department of Health and Care Services Improvement Partnership, 2005). This guide suggests ways of improving mental health and care services for older people. Although it is a number of years old now it is still very useful because it is aimed at practitioners working in health and social care.

CHAPTER SUMMARY

This chapter has introduced you to a number of government strategies and legislation relating to people with dementia and their carers.

The chapter started by examining England's National Dementia Strategy and possible reasons for its development and publication. Then a number of the strategy's objectives were explored with the aim of raising your awareness about the important role of social work and local authorities in putting the strategy into practice. While it was recognised that the strategy was a major step forward in improving the lives of people with dementia and their carers it was also highlighted that certain areas have faced a number of difficulties in the implementation of the strategy. It was then explained that this has resulted in a revised implementation plan being published in 2010.

Next the chapter's focus moved on to the government's guidance on risk enablement. The importance of proportionality in balancing risk was considered.

The chapter then examined the Mental Capacity Act 2005. We discussed the importance of the two-stage test of capacity, in particular the second part of the test that stresses the need for assessment of capacity to be decision- and time-specific. Furthermore we looked at the five key principles of the Act and the importance of considering these alongside the code of practice, in particular in relation to best interests.

We then considered the Human Rights Act 1998 and how it fits into the context of supporting people with dementia. The issue around the interpretation of the term public authority was scrutinised and we considered the possible implications of the case of Mrs YL for social work practice.

Continued

CHAPTER SUMMARY *continued*

You have also been shown some of the other pieces of legislation and strategies that are relevant in supporting people with dementia.

Finally, it is important that as a practitioner you have not only knowledge about the legislation and guidance discussed in this chapter but also the ability to use this knowledge to benefit people with dementia and their carers.

The next chapter will focus on safeguarding and people with dementia. The different categories of abuse will be considered including physical, sexual and institutional abuse. The key pieces of literature and research into abuse and people with dementia will be explored. Finally your role in safeguarding people living with dementia from abuse will be identified.

FURTHER READING

The Alzheimer's Society (2009) *Dementia: What every commissioner needs to know. Guidance on delivering the National Dementia Strategy for England*. London: Alzheimer's Society.

This useful publication has been written to help commissioners of health and social care services to consider the specific needs of people with dementia in relation to the commission of services.

The British Institute of Human Rights (2006) *Your human rights. A guide for older people*. London: The British Institute of Human Rights.

This useful guide provides specific information about older adults and the Human Rights Act (1998). Although it is written for older people it is still useful reading for practitioners involved in supporting people with dementia.

Carruthers, I and Ormondroyd, J (2009) *Age equality in health and social care*. London: The Stationery Office.

This report was written as the result of a request by the Health Secretary to suggest ways of reducing possible age discrimination faced by older adults who use health and social care. It is useful reading as it suggests possible ways of reducing such discrimination.

Department of Health, Social Services and Public Safety (2011) *Improving dementia services in Northern Ireland – A regional strategy*. Belfast: Department of Health, Social Services and Public Safety.

This document describes the drive in Northern Ireland to develop and improve services for people living with dementia. The strategy places a strong emphasis on raising both public and professional awareness of dementia.

Equality and Human Rights Commission (2011) *Close to home: An enquiry into older people and human rights in home care*. London: Equality and Human Rights Commission.

This important document highlights the discrepancy that affects many older adults who receive home care from a private company regarding their human rights. A number of suggestions and arguments are made as to why this needs to be changed, including the possible levels of abuse experienced by older adults in their own home.

Scottish Government (2011) *Scotland's national dementia strategy*. Edinburgh: Scottish Government.

This document describes the Scottish Government's commitment to developing and delivering 'world class' dementia services in Scotland. The strategy has a number of long-term goals, but interestingly it has focused on two key areas to implement change. The first is to make sure that after diagnosis people living with dementia are provided with support and information; and the second is to improve the support given to people with dementia who use general hospitals.

Mental Welfare Commission for Scotland (2011) *Standards of care for dementia in Scotland: Action to support the change programme*. Edinburgh: Scottish Government.

This document has been produced to support the implementation of the Scottish National Dementia Strategy and to highlight the standards that have been developed to help people with dementia and their carers understand their rights. From a practitioner's perspective this document is interesting because it highlights how much further Scotland is on the journey of identifying discrimination against people with dementia and their carers and in suggesting ways of overcoming such discrimination.

Welsh Assembly Government (2011) *National dementia vision for Wales: Dementia supportive communities*. Cardiff: Alzheimer's Society and Welsh Assembly Government.

Four key areas were seen as a priority including: improving service provision across health, social care, the voluntary sector and other agencies; improving early diagnosis and ensuring timely interventions; improving access to information and support for people and ensuring a greater awareness of support services; and improving training for those delivering care. This document is interesting regarding the role of social work because its emphasis is on making changes in the community. Its aim therefore is to create dementia-supportive communities.

USEFUL
WEBSITES

www.dementiauk.org

This is the website for Dementia UK, a national charity that gives more information about the role of Admiral nurses. These are specialist nurses who support carers and families of people with dementia. Dementia UK also has a number of interesting resources for families and practitioners.

www.acting-up.org.uk/opaal

OPAAL stands for Older People's Advocacy Alliance. This useful website provides information about independent advocacy for older people.

www.scie.org.uk

The excellent Social Care Institute for Excellence website has an e-learning resource relating to the Mental Capacity Act. It includes a number of video clips and interactive questions to explore the different elements of the Mental Capacity Act 2005.

www.alzheimers.org.uk/dementiaaction

The Dementia Action Alliance website explains the role of the Dementia Action Alliance. The Alliance is made up of over 80 organisations in the UK who have signed up to a National Dementia Declaration to try and improve services for people with dementia.

Chapter 3
Safeguarding and dementia

Introduction

The chapter begins by defining the different terminology used in safeguarding including *abuse*, *categories of abuse, safeguarding vulnerable adults* and *adults at risk*. Reasons for changes to safeguarding terminology due to the developments in social policy will also be discussed.

Then the chapter briefly summarises some of the policies and legislation in safeguarding, including:

- the Department of Health's *No secrets guidance*;

- the NHS and Community Care Act 1990;

- the Mental Capacity Act 2005; and

- the Human Rights Act 1998.

The second part of the chapter will then examine the research that has been carried out relating to safeguarding people with dementia. In particular we will focus on care homes and hospitals, abuse towards and from family members and the inappropriate use of antipsychotic medication with people with dementia.

In this chapter you will:

- examine the different definitions used in the field of safeguarding adults;

- consider why there have been changes to safeguarding terminology;

- discuss the usefulness of the terms seriousness and proportionality in relation to safeguarding;

- reflect on the importance of the *No secrets* guidance;

- examine different aspects of legislation in relation to safeguarding;

- think about why there is limited research relating to safeguarding people with dementia;

- consider why having a good relationship with care homes is an important aspect in safeguarding people with dementia;

- contemplate the role social workers could have in safeguarding people with dementia from the misuse of antipsychotic medication.

Definitions in safeguarding adults

There are a number of terms and definitions used in safeguarding. This first part of the chapter aims to illustrate the meaning of these terms, starting with defining abuse itself. However, it is important that you as a practitioner recognise that these definitions cannot fully put into words the impact that experiencing or witnessing abuse can have on a person.

What is abuse?

The document *No secrets: Guidance on the protection of vulnerable adults* gives the following definition of abuse:

> *A violation of individuals' human and civil rights by another person or persons.*

> (DoH/Home Office, 2000, p9)

The document also explains that:

> *Abuse may consist of a single act or repeated acts. Abuse can occur in any relationship and may result in significant harm to, or exploitation of, the person subjected to it.*

> (DoH/Home Office, 2000, p9)

This definition is so important because it reminds us that abuse can occur in any relationship and so a perpetrator of abuse can be anyone.

Categories of abuse
No secrets also gives examples of the different categories of abuse including:

- **physical abuse**, *including hitting, slapping, pushing, kicking, misuse of medication, restraint, or inappropriate sanctions;*

- **sexual abuse**, *including rape and sexual assault or sexual acts to which the vulnerable adult has not consented, could not consent or was pressured into consenting to;*

- **psychological abus**e, *including emotional abuse, threats of harm or abandonment, deprivation of contact, humiliation, blaming, controlling, intimidation, coercion, harassment, verbal abuse, isolation or withdrawal from services or supportive networks;*

- **financial or material abuse**, *including theft, fraud, exploitation, pressure in connection with wills, property and inheritance or financial transactions, or the misuse or misappropriation of property, possessions or benefits;*

- **neglect and acts of omission**, *including ignoring medical or physical care needs, failure to provide access to appropriate health, social care or educational services, the withholding of the necessities of life, such as medication, adequate nutrition and heating; and*

- **discriminatory abuse**, *including racist, sexist, that are based on a person's disability, and other forms of harassment, slurs or similar treatment.*

(DoH/Home Office, 2000, p9)

The above categories illustrate the variety of abuse that a person can experience, sometimes experiencing more than one form of abuse (O'Keefe *et al.*, 2007).

Who is a vulnerable adult?

A number of documents, including *No secrets*, developed the term vulnerable adult to describe *an adult aged 18 years or over who is or may be in need of community care services by reason of mental or other disability, age or illness; and who is or may be unable to take care of him or herself, or unable to protect him or herself against significant harm or exploitation* (Lord Chancellor's Department, 1997).

It is important that you are aware of the key definitions and concepts used in safeguarding as it will guide you when you are faced with potential safeguarding issues, as illustrated in the following case study.

CASE STUDY

Loretta is a social work student in her second year. Her placement was at a day centre for people with dementia that was run by the county council. She was enjoying the placement apart from one thing that was making her feel uncomfortable. During her first week at the centre she heard John, a member of staff, calling Daisy, an older adult with dementia, his darling. As he did this he put his arm around her. Daisy pushed him away and protested that, she was nobody's darling. John apologised, saying that he was only trying to give her a 'cuddle'.

ACTIVITY **3.1**

1. Consider what are some of the dilemmas that Loretta may face in this situation.

2. If you were in Loretta's situation what would you do next?

3. Suggest some of the possible indicators, signs and symptoms that could suggest that Daisy is experiencing abuse.

COMMENT

Loretta would need to consider her next steps after witnessing the event. In principle, as part of proving her competence, Loretta should know about the policies and procedures of the organisation she has been placed within, and act upon these accordingly. However, because Loretta is new to the centre she may not have been made aware of these and consequently she may feel unsure about which steps to take. She could speak to her placement supervisor. However, if they were involved in the suspected abuse then Loretta could seek guidance from her university tutor.

Investigating a possible case of abuse

When investigating a possible case of abuse, such as the case of Daisy, an investigating officer will need to consider a number of factors including:

- *Indicators of abuse*. There may be a number of different indicators of abuse. However, just because an individual is showing these does not confirm abuse. Table 3.1 shows a list of possible indicators. It is important to recognise that there are many more possible indicators than the ones listed in the table.

- *The vulnerability of the individual*. In the case study Daisy would be classed as a vulnerable adult because she is *in need of community care services* and has a *disability*, i.e. she has dementia and is attending a day centre. However, just because a person is old or has a disability does not necessarily mean that they are vulnerable. Even with a disability such as dementia some individuals have the mental capacity to make informed choices and decisions about how to protect themselves from abuse and harm. In the case study Daisy seemed to demonstrate the ability to protest against being called 'darling' and being 'cuddled'. However, there may be another time when she does not have the ability to protest against the actions taken by John. This illustrates how important it is to recognise that a person's vulnerability can vary over time and is dependent on many factors.

- *How serious is the abuse*. Assessing how serious abuse is will be a major part in identifying the appropriate response to be taken. In the example given, a person with dementia being called 'darling' and being 'cuddled' may not seem that serious; however, it may be causing the person to experience significant harm. This term is often used to help practitioners assess the seriousness of the abuse and the impact it has on a person. *No secrets* states that *harm should be taken to include not only ill treatment (including sexual abuse and forms of ill treatment which are not physical) but also the impairment of, or an avoidable deterioration in, physical or mental health and the impairment of physical, intellectual, emotional, social or behavioural development* (DoH/Home Office, 2000). This definition stresses the need to consider both the immediate and future impact on the person. In the case example of Daisy the impact on her may not be immediate but it could cause her harm in the longer term.

- *The relevant legislation for guidance*. The action taken needs to be in line with legislation such as the Mental Capacity Act 2005.

A number of other factors would have to be considered including how often the act was occurring, whether or not the law had been broken and *the risk of repeated or increasingly serious acts involving this or other vulnerable adults* (DoH/Home Office, 2000, p12–13).

All of these factors need to be considered to ensure that the response to the concern is *proportionate*. The concept of proportionality has become important as a result of the Human Rights Act 1998. This concept and the Act will be explored in relation to safeguarding later in the chapter.

Table 3.1 Some possible indicators of abuse

Type of abuse	Possible indicators
Discriminatory abuse	• lack of respect shown to an individual • signs of a substandard service offered to an individual • repeated exclusion from rights afforded to citizens such as health, education, employment, criminal justice and civic status • failure to follow the agreed care plans can result in the vulnerable adult being placed at risk
Physical abuse	• any injury not fully explained by the history given • injuries inconsistent with the lifestyle of the vulnerable adult • bruises and/or welts on face, lips, mouth, torso, arms, back, buttocks, thighs • clusters of injuries forming regular patterns or reflecting the shape of an article • burns, especially on soles, palms or back; from immersion in hot water, friction burns, rope or electric appliance burns • multiple fractures • lacerations or abrasions to mouth, lips, gums, eyes, external genitalia • marks on body, including slap marks, finger marks • injuries at different stages of healing • medication misuse
Sexual abuse	• significant change in sexual behaviour or attitude • wetting or soiling • poor concentration • vulnerable adult appears withdrawn, depressed, stressed • unusual difficulty or sensitivity in walking or sitting • torn, stained or bloody underclothing • bruises, bleeding, pain or itching in genital area • sexually transmitted diseases, urinary tract or vaginal infection, love bites • bruising to thighs or upper arms • self-harming behaviour

Continued

Table 3.1 Some possible indicators of abuse continued

Type of abuse	Possible indicators
Psychological abuse	• change in appetite • low self-esteem, deference, passivity and resignation • unexplained fear, defensiveness, ambivalence • sleep disturbance • self-harming behaviour
Financial abuse	• unexplained sudden inability to pay bills or maintain lifestyle • unusual or inappropriate bank account activity • withholding money • recent change of deeds or title of property • unusual interest shown by family or others in the vulnerable adult's assets • person managing financial affairs is evasive or uncooperative
Neglect	• physical condition of the vulnerable adult is poor, e.g. bed sores, unwashed, ulcers • clothing in poor condition, e.g. unclean, wet, ragged • inadequate physical environment • inadequate diet • untreated injuries or medical problems • inconsistent or reluctant contact with health or social care agencies • failure to engage in social interaction • malnutrition when not living alone • inadequate heating • failure of carers to give prescribed medication • poor personal hygiene
Institutional abuse	• inappropriate or poor care • misuse of medication • restraint methods • sensory deprivation, e.g. denial of use of spectacles or hearing aid • lack of respect shown to the vulnerable adult • denial of visitors or phone calls • restricted access to toilet or bathing facilities • restricted access to appropriate medical or social care • failure to ensure appropriate privacy or personal dignity • lack of flexibility and choice, e.g.mealtimes and bedtimes, choice of food • lack of personal clothing or possessions • lack of privacy • lack of adequate procedures, e.g. for medication, financial management • controlling relationships between staff and service users • poor professional practice • high levels of abuse between service users • high turnover of staff or large numbers of agency staff

Source: Sussex multi-agency policy and procedures for safeguarding vulnerable adults (2009, pp40–41). Sussex: Safeguarding Adults Boards of Brighton and Hove, East Sussex and West Sussex.

Changes in terminology

Over the past few years a number of key terms have been developed to reflect changes in public and professional thinking and government policy. An example of such a change is the replacement of the term *adult protection* with the concept of safeguarding.

Adult protection focuses on protecting individuals who are *unable to protect themselves from significant harm* (DoH/Home Office, 2000, s2.3). However, safeguarding differs by promoting the *work which enables an adult to retain independence, well-being and choice and live a life that is free from abuse and neglect. It is about preventing abuse and neglect as well as promoting good practice for responding to concerns on a multi-agency basis* (Newcastle Safeguarding Adults Committee, 2006, p4).

There are a number of reasons behind the change in terminology. These include the following.

- To change the belief that adults need to be protected to one that encourages adults to be supported; to enable them to *retain independence, well-being and choice* and to find ways of empowering the individual to develop the means of reducing the likelihood of abuse occurring. This reflects the concepts behind the personalisation agenda (see Chapter 4).

- To stress the difference between safeguarding and child protection. As the Department of Health stated, *Safeguarding adults is not like child protection. Adults do not want to be treated like children and do not want a system that was designed for children* (DoH, 2009c, p6).

Another term that has caused debate is *vulnerable adult*. The Department of Health's consultation on the *No secrets* guidance found that 90 per cent of respondents wanted the *No secrets* definition of a vulnerable adult either revised or replaced (DoH, 2009c, p8). Consequently some local authorities have started to use the term adult at risk.

ACTIVITY **3.2**

A number of local authorities in England have replaced the term vulnerable adult *with the concept of an* adult at risk*. The term adult at risk is also used in Scotland in the Adult Support and Protection Act 2007, which is discussed later.*

Consider a number of possible reasons why some local authorities in England have started to use the term adult at risk rather than vulnerable adult.

COMMENT

The term adult at risk has been adopted by a number of local authorities for the following reasons.

- *A number of service user organisations felt that the label of* vulnerability *gave the impression that service users were* weak *and* defenceless *and this imagery failed to reflect a number of government documents, including* Our Health, Our Care, Our Say

Continued

(DoH, 2006) and Putting People First *(HM Government, 2007), which promote the independence and empowerment of service users. This change in language also reflects changes in the language of dementia care that encourages those without dementia to think of people with dementia not as sufferers and victims but as unique individuals who still have a significant role to play in society (Moore, 2010, p15).*

- *The term* vulnerable adult *places the emphasis on the person, rather than on the perpetrator of abuse. It can imply that the abuse is a result of something the person who has been abused has done or has not done. As the Association of the Directors of Social Services stated,* the label can be misunderstood, because it seems to locate the cause of abuse with the victim, rather than placing the responsibility with the actions or omissions of others (ADASS, 2005, p4).

- *The definition of vulnerable adult may be seen as too restrictive because of its focus on those in need of community services. The definition of an adult at risk recognises that it is not only people who are in need of community services who may be at risk.*

- *The term adult at risk acknowledges that it is often the situation that a person is in that puts them at an increased risk of abuse. Understanding this can help individuals, working with practitioners and others, to find ways of reducing the likelihood of abuse occurring, for instance, by finding ways to minimise the isolation of a person with dementia who lives in their own home. Other ways of reducing the risk of abuse occurring include the following.*

  - *Education for service users, families and staff across different agencies about the different forms of abuse, signs of abuse and policies and procedures. For instance the Home Office has produced a document,* Keep safe *(Home Office, 2006), designed to help users to increase their awareness about abuse.*

  - *Enabling staff to feel that they can challenge practice that they may see as abusive.*

  - *Supporting advocacy services to help adults at risk to speak up about concerns they have relating to abuse.*

  - *Making sure that information and advice are available for all about safeguarding adults at risk.*

  - *Having an effective recruitment system. The Safeguarding Vulnerable Groups Act 2006 was created after the Bichard Inquiry into the Soham murders. The Act created the Independent Safeguarding Authority which was to oversee a vetting scheme which all individuals who wanted to work with vulnerable groups, such as vulnerable adults, had to undergo. However, the current coalition government undertook a review of the role of the Independent Safeguarding Authority, recommending a merger with the Criminal Records Bureau. The new body will be called the Disclosure and Barring Service and is planned to be in operation by late 2012.*

For this chapter we will continue to use the term vulnerable adult, rather than adult at risk. This is because the term vulnerable adult is still commonly used.

The terminology of safeguarding in adults will probably continue to evolve and change. It is important in your role as a social worker that you understand the different terms and definitions. However, it is equally important to recognise that a number of the people you support may not know what these different terms mean. Consequently it is essential that when you work with service users and their families you do not rely too heavily on safeguarding jargon and terminology.

The *No secrets* guidance

No secrets: Guidance on developing and implementing multi-agency policies and procedures to protect vulnerable adults from abuse was published in 2000. It was jointly produced by both the Department of Health and the Home Office. This is noteworthy because it demonstrated partnership working between agencies, something that should be reflected in safeguarding practice.

Although *No secrets* is not legislation, different agencies, including local authorities, NHS, the police and social care providers, should follow it. In the case of local authorities the guidance is classed as statutory guidance. This is because it was issued under the Local Authority Social Services Act 1970, section 7. This section states that *Local authorities shall, in the exercise of their social services functions, including the exercise of any discretion conferred by any relevant enactment, act under the general guidance of the Secretary of State*.

ACTIVITY *3.3*

Throughout this chapter we have already referred to No secrets *many times. This is because it is arguably the most influential of all the documents relating to the safeguarding of adults. Suggest three reasons why the* No Secrets *guidance has been so important.*

COMMENT

You may have suggested a number of reasons including the following.

- No Secrets *provided a clear definition of the different terms used in safeguarding. This was important because before the guidance various definitions were used by different organisations and this led to inconsistencies in understanding and application.*

- *It has given clear guidelines about how different agencies should work together. In particular it focused on the importance of information sharing.*

- *It placed local authorities in a* co-ordinating role in developing the local policies and procedures for the protection of vulnerable adults from abuse *(DoH/Home Office, 2000, p7).*

- *It introduced the concept of seriousness and extensiveness of abuse. This has been helpful in assessing the level of intervention that should be taken.*

Continued

- *It suggested the development of local adult protection committees. These are now often referred to as Safeguarding Adults Boards. These are boards of various organisations that are involved in safeguarding vulnerable adults.*

Therefore, although this guidance is not a piece of legislation, it has been and still is very important in shaping safeguarding policy and practice.

Consultation on *No secrets*

Since the publication of the *No secrets* guidance there have been many high-profile cases of abuse reported by the media (BBC, *Panorama*, 2011). Such cases, along with changing views about safeguarding, led to calls for a review of the *No secrets* guidance. Consequently the Department of Health launched a consultation process on changes to *No secrets* (Department of Health, 2008b). The findings of the consultation were published in 2009 in *Report on the consultation: The review of No secrets guidance*. The document highlighted a number of key areas that needed to be developed.

Despite this a statement was published by the coalition government in 2011 which announced that *No secrets* would remain as guidance until at least 2013 (Department of Health, 2011a, p4). However, an important element that came out of this statement was the government's intention to make Safeguarding Adults Boards mandatory.

Many still believe that the government needs to go further and introduce specific legislation to safeguard adults from abuse (Action against Elder Abuse, 2011). In Scotland there is legislation for safeguarding adults under the Adult Support and Protection Act 2007.

Adult Support and Protection Act (Scotland) 2007

The Act came about as a result of the Scottish Borders inquiry into the serious abuse of a woman with a learning disability. The Inquiry found that despite concerns having been raised about the woman, no action was taken to safeguard her. The Inquiry suggested a number of recommendations, one being that the Scottish government create legislation to safeguard vulnerable adults.

The Act contains a number of significant elements, including giving local authorities duties and powers in relation to safeguarding adults. These include:

- the power to carry out investigations through visits and interviews;

- the duty to consider the implementation of the appropriate service for the individual, such as an advocate;

- the ability to ask to view different records including financial records. Health records can be requested but they need to be examined by a health professional;

- the co-operation of other agencies with the local authority in making enquiries;
- the ability to apply to a court for different orders including:
  - an assessment order, which involves taking the adult to a suitable place for not more than seven days to assess if they are at risk of abuse;
  - a removal order, which involves taking the person to a suitable place to prevent the individual being harmed;
  - a banning order, to prevent a specified person from having contact with the individual.

Interestingly, the court cannot grant the above orders, except in certain circumstances, without the consent of the adult at risk. This reflects the key principle of the Act, which concerns the empowerment of the individual.

However in England, Wales and Northern Ireland there is no such specific legislation.

ACTIVITY **3.4**

Consider what might be the advantages of having a specific piece of legislation to safeguard adults in England, Wales and Northern Ireland.

COMMENT

You may have considered a number of benefits, including some of those listed below.

- *Local authorities could possibly have a clearer direction on the responses and responsibilities required (Newcastle Safeguarding Adults Committee, 2006, p4). This will be considered further when we look later at the case example of Betty Figg.*
- *Greater emphasis could be placed on all agencies to work together and co-operate, as is the case in Scotland.*
- *There may be increased funding for safeguarding. Underfunding of safeguarding is a common issue. This is due to a number of reasons, including the fact that some safeguarding departments in the country are funded only by adult social services, with no contributions from the police or the NHS (Samuel, 2008, p9). Legislation may bring about equal contributions from different agencies and therefore potentially increase funding.*

However, it is important to reflect that just because legislation is passed does not necessarily mean that the above will occur. Furthermore, there may be benefits from not moving down the legislative route.

Legislation in England

Because there is no specific safeguarding legislation in England it is important that you are aware of the other pieces of legislation that will provide you with a framework to understand the complex world of safeguarding.

NHS and Community Care Act 1990

Section 7 of this Act provides the main tool for practitioners who are safeguarding adults. This is because it places a duty on a local authority to carry out an assessment of need for community services, which can include safeguarding. Safeguarding individuals is a community care service and can be in the form of an assessment of need, organising a service, signposting to a relevant safeguarding organisation or providing information about safeguarding.

The Mental Capacity Act 2005

The Act is relevant to the safeguarding of adults due to a number of key elements.

- First, section 44 of the Act made it a criminal offence to wilfully neglect or ill-treat someone who lacks capacity. This means that anyone who mistreats, neglects or abuses a person who lacks capacity can face criminal charges.

- Second, the Act provided five key principles and Principle 5, the least restrictive intervention, states: *Before the act is done, or the decision is made, regard must be had to whether the purpose for which it is needed can be as effectively achieved in a way that is less restrictive of the person's rights and freedom of action* (MCA 2005, section 1 (6)).

- Third, the Act was amended to include *Deprivation of Liberty Safeguards*. These safeguards require hospitals and care homes to make a request to the local authority for authorisation to deprive a person of their liberty. This means that an individual's liberty cannot be taken away from them without a clear case being presented to show that this is being done in the person's best interests. Refer back to Chapter 2 for more information.

The Human Rights Act 1998

Another key piece of legislation that has shaped safeguarding is the Human Rights Act 1998. This is because it imposes on public authorities (see Chapter 2) a legal duty to uphold the rights of individuals and, as the following from *No Secrets* suggests, *Abuse is a violation of an individual's human and civil rights* (DoH/Home Office, 2000, p7).

The Act has a number of elements that are particularly important for safeguarding adults including:

- Article 3, freedom from torture and cruel, inhuman or degrading treatment or punishment;

- Article 5, right to liberty and security of person; and

- Article 14, prohibition of discrimination.

Sadly there are many examples of cases where these rights have not been respected, in particular concerning people with dementia who have been on hospital wards or in care homes. Examples of these will be considered later in the chapter.

53

The concept of proportionality

Earlier the concept of proportionality was introduced. Local authorities, which are public authorities (see Chapter 2 for a definition of a public authority), have a duty under the Human Rights Act 1998 to *intervene proportionately to protect the rights of citizens*. This means that a public authority has to protect a person's rights in a way that is appropriate and not excessive. In other words, well-intentioned interventions can end up being abusive if the intervention is excessive. However, interpretation of the terms excessive and proportionate is complex and difficult. This is highlighted in the following case study.

CASE STUDY

Betty Figg, April 2009

Betty, an older woman with dementia, was removed from the care home she had been living in for the past year by her daughter, who was concerned that her mother was not receiving appropriate care. However, the daughter's action was against the advice of the older people's mental health team who were involved in Betty's care. Two days after Betty moved into her daughter's home two social workers, accompanied by four police officers and a doctor, removed her from her daughter's property.

The media reported the event using words such as 'snatched' and 'abduction' to describe the actions taken by social services (Daily Mail, 25 April 2009). Pictures featured Betty being taken from the house with a towel over her head and images of police officers with a battering ram. The media also reported Mrs Figg's daughter's view of the situation: No one should be allowed to drag a frail old lady out of her home, away from the family that wants to care for her (Daily Telegraph, 25 April 2009).

ACTIVITY 3.5

From reading the above case example do you think the local authority intervened proportionately to protect Betty Figg? Consider your answer from the perspective of the media, Betty's daughter and the local agencies involved in supporting Betty.

COMMENT

The answer to this is not straightforward. This is because interpretations of the term proportionate will often differ. For example, it seems clear that the media and Betty's daughter saw the actions as excessive.

However, it is reasonable to presume that those agencies involved in removing Betty from her daughter's home saw their actions as proportionate. Legislation was invoked to remove Betty to a place of safety under section 135(1) of the Mental Health Act 1983. This section enables an approved mental health practitioner (or, as it was then, an approved social worker) to:

Continued

make an application for a warrant from a Justice of the Peace which authorises a police officer to enter premises (by force if necessary) where a mentally disordered person is believed to be living and, if thought fit, to remove him/her to a place of safety

and if

it appears to a Justice of the Peace 'that there is reasonable cause to suspect that a person is believed to be suffering from a mental disorder'

(a) has been, or is being, ill-treated, neglected, or kept otherwise than under proper control within the jurisdiction of the justice or

(b) being unable to care for himself, is living alone in any such place.

(Mental Health Act 1983)

Having undertaken such actions it is reasonable to presume that the agencies involved had serious concerns about Betty's welfare. The place of safety would have given those involved in her care an opportunity to assess what steps needed to be taken to safeguard her from harm. In the end the different agencies involved in supporting Betty worked with her daughter to adapt her home to meet Betty's needs. Betty's daughter also went on a course to increase her awareness in supporting a person with dementia. Others also worked with Betty to find out what she wanted to do. This combined effort eventually led to Betty returning to live with her daughter.

However, many would still argue that this was a case of heavy-handedness. Others would state that this is why specific legislation about safeguarding is needed rather than prac-titioners having to piece together different elements of existing legislation to safeguard vulnerable adults. It would be interesting to reflect if a similar situation could have occurred in Scotland where the principles of the Adult Support and Protection Act 2007 provide a statutory framework for local authorities.

Now that we have considered the different definitions, concepts, policies and legislation in safeguarding we will focus in more detail on people with dementia.

People with dementia and safeguarding

At this point it is worth returning to the definition of safeguarding that we referred to at the start of the chapter. This definition demonstrated that safeguarding is about work that enables an adult to retain well-being and choice, and at the same time prevents abuse and neglect. It is not about protecting people to the point where they have no quality of life. This definition of safeguarding is particularly useful when we are considering those living with dementia. This is because, traditionally, people with dementia have been a disempowered population where protection from abuse and risk-taking has often been used as an excuse to control individuals rather than empowering them (Moore, 2010, p34).

Approaches have started to change by recognising the personalised support that people with dementia need. This has certainly been helped by the legislation and guidance discussed in Chapter 2 including the Mental Capacity Act 2005, the National Dementia Strategy (Department of Health, 2009a) and the document *Nothing ventured, nothing gained* (Department of Health, 2010c).

Prevalence of abuse of people with dementia

Recently there have been a number of high-profile cases that have highlighted the abuse of people with dementia (Boniface, 2009; Deighton, 2009; Brooke, 2010).

CASE STUDY

In 2010 three care workers were found guilty of causing abuse to two people with dementia living in a care home. The carers filmed their actions against the two individuals on a mobile phone. In summarising the case the judge stated that although they were elderly and very ill they still had their dignity. Your job was to provide them with a dignified level of care in the last years of their lives. With these despicable acts of abuse you stripped them of their dignity for your own amusement and gratification. Of those who sat in court today and watched the video footage from your mobile phones, nobody could have failed to be appalled by your sick conduct (Brooke, 2010).

ACTIVITY 3.6

1. *How do you think it would feel to be a social worker involved in the above case?*

2. *What effect do you think being involved in such a case could have on a social worker?*

COMMENT

In your role as a social worker it is probable that you will come across some challenging cases of abuse. It is important to be aware of the impact that working on such cases can have on you. These cases will evoke a range of emotions; however, it is important to make sure that you have support from a team and experience good supervision (Bruce and Austin, 2000, p88).

Considering the growing levels of media attention highlighting the problem of abuse, there has been little research that has focused on the numbers of people with dementia who experience abuse in the UK. Studies have looked at the estimated levels of abuse in older adults in the UK (O'Keefe, *et al.*, 2007) but not specifically in those with dementia. This has meant that: *the numbers of people with dementia who suffer abuse or have their human rights violated cannot be reliably quoted* (Joint Commitee on Human Rights, 2007, p212). However, recent research has focused on the prevalence of financial abuse against people with dementia. This is highlighted in the research summary.

RESEARCH SUMMARY

In 2011 the Alzheimer's Society published. Short changed: Protecting people with dementia from financial abuse (Alzheimer's Society, 2011d). The publication described a survey that found that 15 per cent of carers reported that the person they cared for had been subject to some kind of financial abuse.

The report also stated that people with dementia are at an increased risk of experiencing financial abuse because of their reduced capacity to assess risk relating to finance, an increased reliance on others to manage their money, difficulties with using current ways of managing money (such as chip and pin and internet banking) and difficulty in recognising money.

Finally the report claimed that financial abuse of people with dementia needs to be given a much higher profile by local authorities.

Despite uncertainty about the number of people with dementia who experience different forms of abuse there is growing research to indicate that people with dementia are at a greater risk of abuse (Selwood and Cooper, 2009).

ACTIVITY 3.7

1. *Why do you think there have been so few studies looking at the prevalence rates of abuse towards people with dementia in the UK?*

2. *Why do you think people with dementia may be at a greater risk of experiencing abuse?*

COMMENT

There have been a number of suggestions put forward as to why people with dementia may be especially susceptible to abuse. They include the following reasons.

- *The person may not be aware that they are being abused, either because they do not see the incidents as abuse or they forget that abuse has occurred.*

- *There may be difficulties with communication, preventing the person from telling others about the abuse they are experiencing.*

- People with dementia may be fearful of speaking out in case they are not believed, with the dementia being used as justification for ignoring the complaint *(Alzheimer's Society, 2009, p4).*

- *Others may believe that because a person has dementia they will not be a* credible witness *in a court of law. Consequently allegations made by a person with dementia may not be taken seriously.*

As a result of the above it is even more important that as a social worker you are aware of the signs and symptoms that can indicate that a person with dementia may be experiencing abuse.

Research and safeguarding

Although there is limited research into the prevalence of abuse in people with dementia there have been studies into other areas including the mistreatment of people with dementia in institutions including care homes and hospitals; mistreatment by and towards family members; and mistreatment through the use of antipsychotic medication.

A study of care homes

There is a growing recognition of the excellent care that can be provided for the estimated 244,000 people with dementia living in care homes (Alzheimer's Society, 2007b, p6). However, there is still evidence of abuse occurring. The study, *A home from home,* highlighted this: *There were worrying reports about the lack of respect shown by some staff members to residents with dementia, for example making fun of residents and talking about them in a disparaging way. Other carers reported that residents were treated like objects while personal care tasks were carried out* (Alzheimer's Society, 2007b, p20).

The report suggested a number of reasons for this mistreatment; yet one particular area the report focused on was the lack of support managers received from external agencies. The study found that one-third of care home managers reported receiving no support or very little support from health or social services. This is despite the guidance from the Department of Health which outlines how different services for older people need to work together regarding safeguarding (*Everybody's business: Integrated mental health services for older adults*, Department of Health and Care Services Improvement Partnerships, 2005, p35).

ACTIVITY **3.8**

1. *In your role as a social worker how could you support local care homes?*

2. *Why do you think good relationships with care homes are an important aspect in safeguarding people with dementia?*

COMMENT

In your role it will be essential to develop effective relationships with care homes and their managers for a number of reasons, one being the safeguarding of those with dementia. If you have a good relationship with a care home it is possible that the staff, families, residents and manager may be more open to working together to safeguard vulnerable adults.

Studies of hospitals

The National Dementia strategy (2009) included a specific objective to improve the quality of care for people with dementia in hospitals. This was partly due to a number of reports that had highlighted the mistreatment of people with dementia on hospital wards. A report, *Counting the cost: caring for people with dementia on hospital wards* (Alzheimer's

Society, 2009), raised a number of areas of concern including the increased risk people with dementia faced of becoming malnourished while in hospital. Archibald (2006, p42) argued that this risk of malnutrition is so high because nursing staff are not educated about the extra support people with dementia need with eating and drinking. However, another report suggested that it was not due to a lack of education but rather a case of inadequate numbers of staff to assist people with dementia during meal times (Royal College of Nursing, 2008a).

It is clear that more extensive work needs to be done between agencies to try and find ways of improving the quality of care that people with dementia receive in hospital settings and care homes.

Studies of people with dementia, family carers and abuse

Most of the research has focused on the abuse of people with dementia by professional carers in care homes and hospitals rather than abuse they have experienced in their own home from family members. Concern has been raised about this (Cooper *et al.*, 2009) because it is estimated that:

- 60 per cent of the total population of people with dementia live in their own home or with their family;

- abuse of older adults from family members is much more likely than from professional carers (O'Keefe *et al.*, 2007). If this is reflected in those with dementia then this concern can be understood.

A study by University College London (Cooper *et al.*, 2009) has shed some light on this little-researched area. The research found that 52 per cent of the 220 family members questioned reported mistreating the person with dementia while caring for them in their own home. The different forms of abuse varied from physical, the least reported, to verbal, the most common. However, the number of family members reporting physical abuse was considerably lower than that of a similar report undertaken in the USA (Coyne *et al.*, 1993, p644). This led to the UCL researchers suggesting that their figures were an underestimation. They also suggested that because their study relied on self-reporting, carers might not have wished to disclose the full extent of the abuse.

Another piece of research indicates a link between the demands placed on the carer and the level of abuse experienced by the person with dementia (Buttell, 1999, p230). As Coyne *et al.* (1993) argued, abuse may occur because of the *Relatively high psychological and physical demands placed on family members who care for relatives with dementia* (Coyne *et al.*, 1993, p646).

The above quote demonstrates the stress that family members can be put under when living with a person with dementia.

1. *As a social worker how could you support family members who were experiencing these high psychological and physical demands?*

2. *Regarding the safeguarding of a person with dementia, why do you think it would be important to support family members?*

COMMENT

A key part of the Carers' Strategy is the aim to make sure that carers will be supported to stay mentally and physically well and treated with dignity *(HM Government, 2008, p7). Social workers have a key role in making sure that this becomes a reality for family carers of people with dementia.*

In your role as a social worker there will be many ways of supporting family members, including making carers aware of their right to a carers' assessment (The Carers (Equal Opportunities) Act 2004) and making them aware of the services that are available either from the local authority, the NHS or charities such as the Alzheimer's Society. Another way you could help is by increasing families' awareness about dementia to enable them to become aware of possible interventions to prevent abuse. Research by Hansberry et al. (2005) suggested that such interventions helped reduce the levels of abuse occurring. Williamson and Shaffer (2001) suggested that some family carers may not be aware that their behaviour is abusive; consequently education about abuse could also be a key part of your role when working with families.

Abuse of the family carer

We have discussed the importance of recognising that people with dementia can be abused by family carers as well as formal carers. Nevertheless it is important to be aware that family carers can also be subject to abuse. Research that has focused on abuse of the family carer by the person with dementia indicates that this may be a common problem. One piece of research suggested that 37 per cent of family carers interviewed had experienced abuse from the person with dementia within the past three months; 6 per cent said that they had been hit or slapped by the person with dementia (Cooper *et al.*, 2010, pp592–6).

Consider what local authorities could do to raise awareness of abuse of family carers.

COMMENT

Earlier in the chapter we discussed how many local authorities, instead of using the term vulnerable adult, *prefer the concept of an* adult at risk. *One of the key reasons for making this change was to increase awareness among practitioners that carers can*

Continued

experience abuse from the person they are caring for and therefore can be defined as an adult at risk*. As Manthorpe and Iliffe (2009) highlighted:* Older people who are family carers are frequently those who occupy vulnerable positions in caring relationships *(Manthorpe and Iliffe, 2009, p63).*

Local authorities could also make practitioners aware of this issue through training, discussions in team meetings and during supervision. Decisions could be made as to whether or not practitioners should be asking carers if they are experiencing abuse themselves, as suggested from research undertaken by Cooper et al. *(2010, p595). Such questioning would have to be handled very sensitively and even then a person may not openly acknowledge that they are being abused due to a number of factors including fearing that the person with dementia may be taken away from them.*

People with dementia and antipsychotics

No secrets (DoH/Home Office, 2000) gives the misuse of medication as an example of physical abuse. A category of drugs that seems to be misused and overprescribed in people with dementia is antipsychotics. These drugs are used to 'treat' psychosis and behavioural problems, including aggression and agitation, which can be common in people with dementia (Parnetti, *et al.*, 2001, p2064).

It is estimated that in the UK 180,000 people with dementia are given antipsychotic medication every year (Banerjee, 2009, p3) and these numbers have been steadily increasing (Valiyeva, *et al.*, 2008, p442). However, there is growing concern that these drugs are being inappropriately prescribed to people with dementia (All-Party Parliamentary Group on Dementia, 2008) and in the majority of cases the harm caused by antipsychotics outweighs the benefits (Department of Health, 2010b, p10).

International research has highlighted the serious problems that antipsychotic use can cause in people with dementia, including accelerating cognitive decline, increasing the risk of falls and increasing the risk of death in people with dementia (Schneider *et al.*, 2005, p1934; Banerjee, 2009, p3). In spite of these risks *antipsychotics still appear to be used all too often, in secondary as well as primary care, as a formulaic first line response to any behavioural difficulty in dementia rather than as a considered second line treatment when other approaches have failed* (Banerjee, 2009, p30).

In 2010 the government recognised the need to reduce the use of antipsychotics. In a significant move it made the reduction in the use of antipsychotics for people with dementia one of its four priorities in a revision of the National Dementia Strategy.

ACTIVITY 3.11

Consider what role social workers could have in safeguarding people with dementia from the misuse of antipsychotic medication.

COMMENT

The role of the social worker in safeguarding people with dementia from the misuse and overprescribing of these drugs is still unclear. It is possible that social workers could be instrumental in:

- *helping other practitioners consider the range of ethical issues that need to be addressed when looking at the use of these drugs. For example, if a person with dementia does not have mental capacity then the principles of the Mental Capacity Act 2005 should be followed. For instance, prescribing these drugs must be in the person's best interests and be the option that is least restrictive of the person's rights and freedoms;*

- *suggesting possible social and psychological reasons for the behaviour being shown by the person with dementia and therefore potentially finding solutions to the behaviour;*

- *continuing to suggest alternatives to antipsychotics;*

- *demonstrating to other agencies what these alternatives are;*

- *reminding other professionals and practitioners why alternatives need to be sought.*

CHAPTER SUMMARY

- This chapter has considered the different definitions and terms used within safeguarding, including the concept of abuse and the categories of abuse according to the *No secrets* guidelines. Furthermore we considered possible reasons for changes in terminology including the need for language that reflects the movement towards personalisation.

- We then explored some of the key legislation and policies relating to safeguarding including *No secrets*, the Mental Capacity Act 2005 and the Human Rights Act 1998.

- Next the chapter focused on the high number of cases of abuse of people with dementia that are being reported by the media. The chapter also asked you to consider reasons why, despite these high-profile cases, the amount of data in this area is still limited.

- This chapter has also sought to develop your knowledge about the mistreatment that people with dementia can receive, both in care homes and on hospital wards, as well as encourage you to consider ways in which you could work with care home managers in relation to safeguarding.

- The issue of abuse by family members was emphasised as well as the abuse carers themselves can experience. Finally the use of antipsychotic medication with people with dementia was acknowledged.

- In conclusion, when safeguarding people with dementia it is key to remember the definition of safeguarding that was considered in this chapter. Your role is one of empowering the person with dementia to live well with dementia, as well as preventing and protecting the person from harm. The danger

Continued

CHAPTER SUMMARY

is that we see the label of 'dementia' and use this as an excuse to overprotect the person rather than safeguard the person. The essential ingredient when working with people with dementia is to be aware that safeguarding is as much about empowerment as it is about protection.

- The next chapter goes on to to consider how the personalisation agenda is being used to transform services in health and social care. The process of self-directed support will be examined including the different elements of this process such as personal budgets, direct payments and self-assessment. Chapter 4 will also consider the personalisation agenda and its part in promoting the well-being of people with dementia.

FURTHER READING

Alzheimer's Society (2009) *Counting the cost: Caring for people with dementia on hospital wards.* London: Alzheimer's Society.

This report provides an interesting insight into the experience of people with dementia on hospital wards. It highlights the variation in treatment of people with dementia across England, Wales and Northern Ireland.

Association of Directors of Social Services (ADASS) (2005) *Safeguarding adults: A national framework of standards for good practice and outcomes in adult protection work.* London: ADASS.

This important document highlights the importance of viewing vulnerable adults as central to the safeguarding process. It provides 11 standards of good practice relating to safeguarding. A useful collection of examples of good practice is used throughout the document.

Mantell, A and Scragg, T (2011) *Safeguarding adults in social work.* 2nd edition. Exeter: Learning Matters.

This excellent book covers a wide range of areas relating to safeguarding, from looking at the importance of effective collaborative working to considering the link between policy and practice.

Welsh government (2000) *In safe hands: Implementing adult protection procedures in Wales.* Cardiff: National Assembly for Wales.

This document was produced by the Welsh Government shortly after the publication of *No secrets* and is Wales's equivalent to *No secrets*. It is worth reading to see the framework that was proposed for Wales. As with *No secrets*, *In safe hands* recently went through a review.

USEFUL WEBSITES

www.elderabuse.org.uk

This website details the role of the charity Action on Elder Abuse, providing a valuable range of information. It also includes a helpline: 0808 808 8141.

www.panicoa.org.uk

This is the website of Preventing Abuse and Neglect in Institutional Care of Older Adults (PANICOA). It gives details about research that is looking at abuse and neglect in institutional settings. The research is jointly funded by the Department of Health and Comic Relief.

www.inpea.net

This interesting website for the International Network for the Prevention of Elder Abuse provides a useful awareness-raising toolkit that can be used in different settings. It also gives useful information about international awareness campaigns such as World Elder Abuse Awareness Day, which is on 15 June every year.

Chapter 4
Personalisation and dementia

Introduction

One of your key roles as a social worker will be enabling the personalisation of services to become a reality for all people who use services, including those living with dementia.

In this chapter you will look at the concept of personalisation and how it has been viewed as the main catalyst to transform health and social care services to enable: *every person who receives support to have choice and control over the shape of that support* (Department of Health, 2006).

You will consider the different ways in which this agenda is changing social care services, through direct payments, personal budgets, self-assessment and support planning. (These tools are being used to give individuals the opportunity to assess their own needs as well as decide how to spend their allocated money to meet these needs.)

The chapter will also demonstrate ways in which self-directed support, the process being used by local authorities to implement transformation, is being used to promote the personalisation of services for people living with dementia. The obstacles that people with dementia and their carers face when trying to access self-directed support are also explored including the barrier of limited public and professional awareness about the suitability of self-directed support for people with dementia. Finally, possible solutions to these barriers are examined, including considering the skills needed by social workers to make personalisation work for people with dementia and their carers.

This chapter will help readers to:

- consider the concept of personalisation;

- examine how local authorities are implementing the personalisation agenda through self-directed support;

- reflect upon how the personalisation agenda is influencing the role of social workers;

- contemplate how self-directed support is being used with people living with dementia;

- be aware of some of the boundaries people living with dementia face regarding self-directed support and how these obstacles are being overcome.

We shall start by examining the personalisation agenda.

The personalisation agenda

In 2006 the White Paper, *Our health, our care, our say: A new direction for community services* (DoH, 2006) was published. This paper set out the government's view of the direction that health and social care should take towards personalisation of services, known as the personalisation agenda. The aim of the agenda is to move services provided by health and social care away from the control of professionals towards those who use a service. As Carr states: *Personalisation means thinking about care and support services in an entirely different way. This means starting with the person as an individual with strengths, preferences and aspirations and putting them at the centre of the process of identifying their needs and making choices about how and when they are supported to live their lives* (Carr, 2010, p3).

Within social care services self-directed support is being used as the main process to implement the personalisation of services and replace care management.

ACTIVITY 4.1

Imagine you are meeting a person who uses services. They want to know why social services need to change. What would you say to them?

COMMENT

These changes have come about after many years of campaigning from people about the inadequacy of the services they use (Carr, 2010, p61). In addition the need for change in supporting people with dementia has come about as a result of the promotion of person-centred care (see Chapter 1) and the publication of numerous reports highlighting inadequacies in current services for people living with dementia (see Chapter 2).

Continued

COMMENT *continued*

Change has also occurred in response to a number of pieces of literature and policy that have focused on the need for reform, including the government document Putting people first: a shared vision and commitment to the transformation of adult social care *(HM Government, 2007).*

Self-directed support: The aim to empower

There is a long history in this country of users of services being disempowered both by society and by the services that they use (Carr, 2010, p61). Hence self-directed support has been seen as a way of empowering people. The Association of Directors of Adult Social Services (ADASS) has suggested a number of ways that self-directed support can do this.

- First a person can assess his or her own needs through a *self-assessment*. The reasoning behind this is that a person will know their own needs and circumstances better than anyone else. This is different from a traditional assessment of needs where the social worker and other professionals would control the content of the assessment. Although a good assessment would have been person centred (focus on the service user) it would not have been person led (the content controlled by the service user). As a social worker you will still have to carry out a person's assessment of needs for community care services in accordance with the NHS and Community Care Act 1990.

- Second a person is made aware of the amount of money they will have to spend on helping meet their outcomes. An outcome is something a person aims to achieve that will improve their social care needs. Traditionally the amount of money spent on a service would not be shared with a person or their family.

- Next a person would write his or her own plan of support. If the person needs help this can come from family members, their social worker, independent agencies or whoever is deemed suitable to do this. The plan would describe how a person was going to use their allocated money to meet their outcomes. Traditionally the social worker would have written an individual's care plan (ADASS, 2009, pp3–4).

ACTIVITY **4.2**

The verb to care is defined as to provide, look after, and watch over. *To support is defined as* to back up, to nourish, to strengthen *(Chambers' Twentieth Century Dictionary, 2008).*

- *Consider these two definitions; why do you think the terminology has changed from 'care plan' to 'support plan'?*

- *What do you think are the key differences between a 'care plan' and a 'support plan'?*

COMMENT

As previously discussed the personalisation agenda is about putting people in control of their lives, enabling them to identify and manage their own needs. Traditionally care plans have been completed by professionals who have identified the individual's needs on their behalf. The care plan is often prescriptive as to the service provision the individual will receive, for example, stating the number of hours of care an individual requires.

A support plan should put control firmly with the individual. It moves away from being professional led to person led. However, the professional's role is still fundamental in providing the relevant advice and support to the individual to enable them to develop a plan that achieves their preferred or desired outcomes.

Personal budgets

Once the plan has been agreed a person is given their personal budget. A personal budget is *the amount of money that will fund a person's care and support costs. It is calculated by assessing a person's needs. It is spent in line with a support plan that has been agreed by both the person and the council* (ADASS, 2009, p4).

Before the advent of self-directed support an individual would have had very little choice or control over how the money for social care, provided by their council, was used.

Receiving a personal budget

A person's budget can be received in a number of ways including through a direct payment. Since 2003 every council in England has had a duty to offer individuals who are eligible a direct payment. With a direct payment a person's pot of money (their personal budget) is paid directly from the council to the person's bank account. The individual can then use this money to make arrangements to find ways of meeting their needs.

Through a direct payment a person can decide how their outcomes will be met by arranging their own support. For instance a person living with dementia may find that home care workers provided by the council cannot visit at a time that is suitable for them. Through a direct payment the person could employ someone to come at a time that is convenient for them. The local authority will need to agree that the money is being spent in a way that meets the individual's outcomes.

Alternatively the council can undertake the role of managing the money and finding suitable providers or place the money with an organisation that can manage a person's budget for them.

Ian was diagnosed with fronto-temporal dementia when he was 54. He lives with his wife Jennifer. Although Jennifer continued to work after Ian was diagnosed, she eventually had to take early retirement from her job in retail to care for him.

Jennifer contacted her local adults' services department and was visited by a social worker. After initial assessments it was decided that Ian would be eligible for a service. A social worker discussed the self-directed support process with Jennifer. However, Jennifer felt that Ian did not have the ability to manage a direct payment himself. Consequently Jennifer was assessed by the council as a suitable person to receive the direct payment on Ian's behalf.

After advertising for a personal assistant in her local paper she found two individuals whom she now employs to support Ian. With the support of a local agency and Ian's social workers, Jennifer manages the required paperwork and deals with the payments from the council.

Until recently a person who could not give their consent was not able to receive a direct payment. (Section 57 of the Health and Social Care Act 2001 required a service user to 'consent' to receiving direct payments.) This ruled out a number of people with dementia from receiving a direct payment. However, changes to legislation in 2009 meant that a suitable individual could be chosen to receive these payments on the person's behalf. This has meant that direct payments can be open to many more people with dementia via a suitable person. In the case study, Jennifer was able to act as a suitable person for Ian. This meant that Ian and Jennifer could decide to meet Ian's social care needs by employing personal assistants. Before 2009 Ian would have had his choice of services limited to those provided by his local council.

2003: *In Control established itself as a social enterprise. In Control goes on to pioneer the use of self-directed support.*

Direct payments guidance: Community care, services for carers and children's services (direct payments) guidance (DoH, 2003).

Social workers have a duty to offer a direct payment to individuals who are eligible and have capacity to manage their payments (with or without assistance). However, this changed in 2009 when new legislation was introduced. These changes meant that a person without capacity could be offered a direct payment via a 'suitable' person.

2006: *The White Paper Our health, our care, our say is published. This document highlights the need for making services flexible and responsive to the needs of service users.*

2007: *Putting people first was published explaining the government's vision for personalising social care to enable individuals a greater choice and control over the services they use.*

Continued

2008: *13 sites across England are chosen to pilot self-directed support. The evaluation of the pilots is published (Individual Budgets Evaluation Network (IBSEN, 2008).*

2009: *The National Dementia Strategy is published. This document contains 17 objectives, which aim to transform the lived experience of people with dementia. Objective 6 concentrates on improving social care support:* Provision of an appropriate range of services to support people with dementia living at home and their carers. Access to flexible and reliable services, ranging from early intervention to specialist home care services, which are responsive to the personal needs and preferences of each individual and take account of their broader family circumstances. Accessible to people living alone or with carers, people who pay for their care privately, through personal budgets, or through local authority-arranged services *(Department of Health, 2009a, p46).*

November 2009: *The duty of social workers to offer a direct payment is extended to eligible adults who lack capacity. The payment can now be given to a 'suitable person' who receives and manages the payments on behalf of the person who lacks capacity.*

2011: *Local authorities should have met National Indicator 130 – 'social care clients receiving self-directed support'. The target was for 30 per cent of people using social services to have self-directed support.*

The role of social workers in implementing self-directed support

During the initial introduction of self-directed support there was concern about what would be the role, if any, of social workers (Ivory, 2008). Despite these initial concerns there is growing evidence to suggest that the role of social workers is essential in making self-directed support work (Tyson, 2009) even though the role itself may be changing. In fact it has been argued that self-directed support has given social workers the opportunity to return to the origins of good social work practice. As Carr (2010) pointed out, positive social work practice has always emphasised the need to put the person first through person-centred care planning, independent living and empowerment.

When you are a social worker, your role will involve working closely with service users and their families to enable them to have greater control and choice.

John, an older adult with dementia, had been visiting a local-authority-run day centre once a week. However, he had become increasingly unhappy at the centre and had decided he would no longer go.

Continued

At John's review the social worker explained that self-directed support had recently been introduced and suggested to John and his wife that this would give them a wider choice of options.

Working with John and his wife the social worker enabled John to receive a personal budget. The money was used to employ a personal assistant who accompanied John to the British Legion, an organisation that John had engaged with before his diagnosis.

John's budget was quite small and he could only afford to pay the personal assistant to accompany him twice a week. However, he soon started to go five times a week because an old friend from the Legion was happy to take him three times a week.

As you can see from this example, John was able to use the money he received from the council (his personal budget) to employ a personal assistant. This enabled him to visit a club he found more suitable to his needs. The case study also shows you the key role a social worker has in supporting a person with dementia and their carer through the self-directed support process, offering guidance and advice.

Self-directed support and people with dementia

In 2008 a report was published that reviewed self-directed support in 13 local authorities across England (the Individual Budgets Evaluation Network (IBSEN)). This report suggested that certain groups of people involved in the pilots, including people with dementia, did not want the extra responsibilities that self-directed support brought with it.

However, research by Kinnaird (2010) has indicated that this is not the case and in fact people living with dementia are willing to be involved in the self-directed support process and can gain a number of benefits including:

* a greater level of flexibility;

* the opportunity for choice and control over how support is provided;

* the ability of family carers to respond to crisis situations;

* being supported at home rather than in a care home (Kinnaird, 2010, p29).

The study did find that the uptake of direct payments by people living with dementia was low yet they argued this was because councils were not promoting the use of direct payments for people living with dementia. Interestingly the study found that more than half of the people questioned had heard about direct payments from sources such as family or friends rather than from the local authority. This finding was mirrored in work by Lightfoot: *Talking to carer groups throughout the region, the message was clear, very few had heard of or been offered a Personal budget /Direct payment for the person they are* caring for. Many displayed a real sense of anger and frustration that this form of support had not been offered, some even saying they would not have moved the person they cared for into residential care if they had been offered a Personal budget (Lightfoot, 2010, p9).

People with dementia: a greater need for self-directed support?

It has been argued that a flexible personalised approach, that could be achieved through self-directed support, is essential for people with dementia. As Lightfoot described: *the support that a person experiencing dementia needs, can differ greatly from one day to the next. That's why conventional support arranged by the Local Authority does not always work, it's often not flexible enough or able to offer the type of person centred care that is needed to prevent hospital admissions and premature moves into residential care* (Lightfoot, 2010, p3).

ACTIVITY 4.3

It could be argued that for people with dementia the need to have personalised services is greater than for many other service user groups. Do you believe there is a greater need of personalised services for people with dementia? If so, why?

COMMENT

A potential reason why people living with dementia have a greater need is because, unlike other groups of individuals, their views have not been widely advocated. This has partly been because it was presumed that people with dementia could not voice their views and opinions due to cognitive difficulties such as short-term memory loss (Moore, 2010, p24). However, it has also been because legislation has often focused on people with learning or physical disabilities. For instance, although direct payments were introduced for these two groups of users in 1996 (The Community Care, Direct Payments Act) these payments were not extended to older people until 2003. Even when direct payments were available to all groups there were still inconsistencies. A report by the old inspection body, the Commission for Social Care Inspection (CSCI) found that there was an underinvestment in promoting direct payments for older people compared to people with physical disabilities. This was despite older people accounting for over 60 per cent of total expenditure by local authorities (CSCI, 2008b).

These inconsistencies should not apply to self-directed support. As Lightfoot points out, *there are no exclusions relating to diagnosis, age etc, therefore people living with dementia are intended to be fully included in self direct support* (Lightfoot, 2010, p3). However, the question is: are people living with dementia receiving the full benefits of self-directed support?

Obstacles to using self-directed support for people with dementia

Research has suggested that there are a number of obstacles for people living with dementia regarding the use of self-directed support (Mental Health Foundation, 2011). Moore and Jones (2011) claimed that these barriers have developed because self-directed support has not been heavily promoted for people with dementia as highlighted in the earlier work of Kinnaird (2010) and Lightfoot (2010). They suggested that this was because of the assumptions made by some practitioners that people with dementia do not have the ability nor the interest to undertake the process. They go further to suggest that these assumptions may lead to those living with dementia not being fully informed about the advantages of receiving a personal budget through a direct payment.

Lightfoot (2010) suggested that practitioners are still not feeling confident in offering self-directed support. She also suggested that some practitioners were not fully aware of the changes to the direct payment regulations and guidance in relation to capacity. Accordingly they were not offering direct payments as an option for people living with dementia.

However, it is not only the view of some practitioners that is contorted. When you are working with people living with dementia you may find that they believe that undertaking a direct payment is too complex and time-consuming. Research by Moore and Jones (2011) indicated that a number of individuals living with dementia in their local authority believed that receiving a personal budget via a direct payment would be too difficult. A review of self-directed support by Alzheimer Scotland also found that many of the carers spoken to believed that the self-directed support process was full of red tape (Kinnaird, 2010, p35).

ACTIVITY **4.4**

Imagine you are a practising social worker who is visiting a person with dementia and their partner. The person with dementia is eligible for support from the council.

Consider the following questions.

- *What might be the positives of self-directed support?*

- *What might be some of the issues?*

In your role as a social worker, how could you promote the positives and overcome some of these issues?

COMMENT

There are many ways that you could promote the positives of self-directed support for people with dementia. For instance, you could make your colleagues and other practitioners aware of the growing material that demonstrates these benefits. For example, you could direct them to the following Mental Health Foundation website: www.mental-health.org.uk/. This website includes numerous video clips and training materials about self-directed support and dementia.

Other issues for people with dementia using self-directed support

Other potential issues for people living with dementia using self-directed support include the following:

- There can be difficulties finding and employing staff including personal assistants.

- The system is too slow from initial contact by the person living with dementia to payment.

- A person with dementia may say that they do not need help when they do.

- There may be issues concerned with eligibility criteria and lack of early intervention (Kinnaird, 2010, p4).

Other potential obstacles are highlighted in the following research summary.

RESEARCH SUMMARY

In 2008 the Mental Health Foundation carried out a survey looking at the use of direct payments for people with early onset dementia (people under the age of 65). The Foundation contacted 40 local authorities by telephone, asking to speak to someone about direct payments for a younger person with dementia. Only five of the 40 authorities connected the caller to the correct department to deal with direct payments. When the caller finally reached the right person or department they found that nearly half of those questioned were not aware that younger people could have dementia (Mental Health Foundation, 2008).

Self-directed support may be particularity beneficial for younger people with dementia. This is because currently there is a shortage of services for this group (Cox and Keady, 1999, p203). Consequently many younger people find themselves receiving services intended for older people.

However, as the research suggests, there is a greater need for awareness about younger people with dementia. It also highlights some of the difficulties that people can face when trying to contact their local authority.

Despite these obstacles there is growing evidence that self-directed support works incredibly well with people living with dementia *if* the obstacles and barriers are overcome. This is illustrated by the following quotes from family carers of people with dementia who are using self-directed support.

> *I feel for me it has been a complete lifeline because I think I am someone who likes to have a certain amount of control to what is happening to us.*

> *I think being given the choice between having direct payments where I could choose the people you felt had the right chemistry versus being given whatever was available . . . I wouldn't have been happy with that.*

> *I now have control over who comes through my front door.*

> *It has provided me with the flexibility to try and create a quality of life for Ian in terms of having people he enjoys being with and shares interests.*

When you live with somebody with dementia you naturally slow down. Controlling the budget has helped me to keep my mind active.

We got mum back, mum with Alzheimer's, but we got mum back.

We advertised for a personal assistant. Alison came and she was heaven. She came for an interview and the first thing she said to me was would I be able to sit with your mum for a while . . . she sat with mum and mum put her hand out to hold Alison's hand. I thought, you have just accepted her, mum, so we will accept her as well.

(Moore and Jones, 2011, p27)

Social work practitioners are also reporting the benefits as highlighted in the following.

I worked with a woman with vascular dementia who was about to lose her warden assisted accommodation due to her restlessness and anxiety at night time. We set up direct payments, via her son, which they used to buy in a package of homecare to ensure she was having lots of social contact, 1–1 time and reassurance, especially in the evenings. The care workers were able to respond to her needs far more flexibly than with care management due to the focus on outcomes rather than tasks. For example, they took her out to a farm so that she could see some owls, which are her favourite animals, they also went out on drives along the coast, which she hadn't been able to do for years. The son has also 'topped-up' the hours we were able to provide and she has been able to go to lots of different places every day – she's still in her flat, her distress is much reduced and she is much happier.

(Moore and Jones, 2011, p27)

Overcoming the obstacles faced by people with dementia

Alzheimer Scotland suggested a number of key ways of overcoming some of the potential obstacles faced by people living with dementia when they are trying to access self-directed support. They included the following suggestions.

- Increase potential recipients' awareness through publicity and impartial information, so that people with dementia and their carers are aware of what is involved.

- Improve understanding within social work departments towards direct payments and their potential benefit for people with dementia.

- Eligibility should be from the onset of diagnosis. Managing a small budget at the early stage of dementia may enable people to become more familiar with the process and better able to manage larger and more complex packages later on.

- Offer a range of support services such as a broker, who can support people to find the right support for their individual needs (Kinnaird, 2010, pp49–51).

These options, although valid, will take time for implementation. Thus the role of the social worker is crucial in enabling people living with dementia to overcome barriers.

Henry Simmons, chief executive of Alzheimer Scotland, said the benefits of direct payments remained a well-kept secret for people with dementia and that Availability of direct payments is being filtered through the systemic assumption that this approach is unrealistic.

In your role as a social worker, how would you make sure that direct payments did not remain a well-kept secret for people living with dementia? Think about how you could work with:

- *people with dementia and their families;*

- *your colleagues in social care;*

- *different agencies including health and the voluntary sector.*

COMMENT

The key to overcoming these issues lies in the skill of the social worker. You will need to use your skills as a social worker to make sure that those living with dementia can truly benefit from self-directed support and be fully informed about how it can help them. The skills you will need include the following.

- *You must have the ability to build a relationship of trust between yourself and a person with dementia and their families. This trust is essential for people with dementia, who rely so heavily on their emotional memories. (Moore, 2010, p51)*

- *You need to be able to use active listening skills to hear a person's story. This is so important for people with dementia, who may not have a real opportunity to express their views.*

- *You must be able to identify the preferred way the person with dementia communicates and understand the importance of your own verbal and non-verbal communication.*

- *You should use language that a person living with dementia can understand. The amount of jargon and acronyms used in self-directed support can be overwhelming for practitioners let alone people using services.*

CHAPTER SUMMARY

This chapter has introduced you to the personalisation agenda, specifically self-directed support, and its influence on people living with dementia.

The first section of the chapter considered the different aspects of self-directed support including the importance of self-assessment, personal budgets and how a person can receive their budget. Furthermore the differences between a traditional care plan and a support plan were examined.

Continued

CHAPTER SUMMARY *continued*

Next the chapter highlighted the reforms that have led to the introduction of the personalisation agenda including the National Dementia Strategy and *Putting people first*.

The chapter went on to consider how the role of social workers is changing because of self-directed support. It was concluded that many people see personalisation as an opportunity to return to the fundamental elements of social work practice.

The next part of this chapter looked at research that has focused on the use of self-directed support by people living with dementia. The existing research has highlighted the low numbers of people living with dementia who use direct payments.

Furthermore it has identified some of the obstacles encountered by people living with dementia who use or aim to use self-directed support. Key concepts of how to overcome these obstacles were suggested. Finally the chapter has highlighted the need for social workers to utilise their skills in overcoming these obstacles to ensure that the personalisation agenda becomes and remains a reality for people with dementia.

Despite the proposed changes needed to overcome the obstacles people with dementia face, Moore and Jones (2011) argue that:

> *For transformation of services to truly happen there needs to be a fundamental shift in how people without dementia see people with dementia. It does not matter how much social care changes its structures and paperwork, if staff do not see the person as an individual with skills and knowledge who has the ability to take control of their life despite the difficulties they face because of having dementia, then nothing will change.*

> (Moore and Jones, 2011, p28)

It is this that is key in your role as a social worker and to the success of self-directed support; to truly see all service users you support as unique individuals.

The next chapter will focus on different ways of promoting independence for people with dementia through reablement services and assistive technology. You will consider the different models of reablement and the differences between each. You will also consider the benefits and issues concerned with using assistive technology to support people living with dementia.

FURTHER READING

Falloon, M, Fowler, D and Prentice, S (2010) *Support planning and brokerage service for older people: Self directed support*. London: Age UK.

This very useful toolkit consists of a booklet, which describes the partnership between Age UK and the local authority in Bromley, and a DVD. Both give the views of older people using services.

Alzheimer's Society (2011) *Getting personal'? Making personal budgets work for people with dementia*. London: Alzheimer's Society.

This fascinating survey of 1,432 people with dementia and carers living in the community found that less than 40 per cent of those questioned have been offered a personal budget. The report calls for changes to be made to the current system to make it appropriate for people with dementia.

Carr, S (2010) *Personalisation: A rough guide*. London: Social Care Institute for Excellence.

This guide provides an explanation of personalisation and gives practical examples of how personalisation has been implemented in certain areas of the country. The guide also gives a clear description of the different terms used within the personalisation agenda.

Department of Health (2010) *Putting people first: Personal budgets for older people – making it happen*. London: Department of Health.

This significant guide is useful reading because it has been written by the Department of Health specifically for councils and their partners. The guide gives a diverse range of examples of how personalisation is being developed with older adults.

Kinnaird, L (2010) *Let's get personal – personalisation and dementia*. Edinburgh: Alzheimer Scotland.

This research gives a significant scoping of the use of personal budgets by people living with dementia in Scotland. The study involved interviewing those living with dementia who were using direct payments. It identifies crucial barriers to the implementation of personalisation.

Moore, D and Jones, K (2011) Making personalisation work for people with dementia. *Journal of Dementia Care*, 19(1), 26–28.

The article explores how self-directed support has been implemented within West Sussex. The authors discuss some of the obstacles faced and how the council is responding to these challenges.

Jutlla, K and Moreland, N (2008) The personalisation of dementia services and existential realities: Understanding Sikh carers caring for an older person with dementia in Wolverhampton. *Journal of Ethnicity and Inequalities in Health and Social Care*, 2(4), 10–21.

This interesting piece of research highlights the difficulties Asian carers have in accessing services when caring for a person with dementia. The paper discusses possible reasons for this in relation to a group of Sikh carers living in Wolverhampton.

USEFUL WEBSITES

www.alzscot.org

The Alzheimer Scotland website is an excellent resource with sections about personalisation and dementia. The website also includes documents about personalisation and living with dementia that can be downloaded.

www.mentalhealthfoundation.org.uk

This website reports on the Mental Health Foundation's study into the use of self-directed support by people with dementia, *Dementia Choices*. The website has a wealth of information and downloadable documents about self-directed support and people with dementia.

Chapter 5
Promoting independence for people with dementia

Introduction

It is estimated that two-thirds of all people with dementia live in their own homes in the community; this is approximately 500,000 people (Alzheimer's Society, Jan 2010e). The Alzheimer's Society believe that many people with dementia wish to remain in their own home for as long as possible and be able to make choices about their lifestyle. The National Dementia Strategy identified that people with dementia require a range of services to enable them to achieve this as outlined in Objective 6: Improved community personal support services (DoH, 2009a).

Furthermore the strategy has also identified the potential for assistive technology to support the needs of people with dementia and their carers. This is outlined in Objective 10: Considering the potential for housing support, housing-related services and telecare to support people with dementia and their carers (DoH, 2009a).

As well as the benefits to people with dementia themselves of continuing to live independently, there are also economic benefits that can be achieved through the reduction in the immediate need of long-term care services.

This chapter explores how people with dementia can be empowered to maintain their independence and continue to live in their own homes. The chapter will look first at reablement services as part of the transforming adult care agenda. We shall consider the model of reablement services while identifying how they can enable people with dementia to continue to be independent and utilise their skills and abilities.

Furthermore, intermediate care is explored to help clarify how this service differs from reablement. In addition we shall consider how accessible intermediate care is for people with dementia.

The chapter will then go on to consider the potential of housing options and the growing use of assistive technology and reflect on its appropriate use for people with dementia.

This chapter will help readers to:

- consider models of reablement services;

- reflect upon the differences between reablement and intermediate care services;

- be aware of the boundaries people living with dementia may be faced with when accessing reablement and intermediate care services;

- contemplate how reablement services can empower people with dementia to remain independent;

- review the potential housing options that can contribute towards enabling independence for people with dementia;

- examine the use of assistive technology in enabling independence for people with dementia;

- reflect on the ethical issues regarding the use of assistive technology for people with dementia.

Reablement services

Reablement services have emerged as a result of the government's directive on transforming adult care. With a focus on personalising services there has been an increased move towards providing prevention and early intervention services. The Department of Health in agreement with the Association of Directors of Adult Social Services (ADASS) and the Local Government Association (LGA) identified five key priorities during the first phase of transformation. Reablement contributes directly to one of these priorities – prevention and cost-effective services (Joint Improvement Partnership South East, 2010).

The Joint Improvement Partnership South East identify that *Reablement services play an important role in delivering early intervention and prevention services by assisting people who need a little help at an early stage to stay independent for as long as possible* (Joint Improvement Partnership South East, 2010, p3).

The Care Services Efficiency Delivery (CSED) programme helps local authorities to identify and develop more efficient ways of delivering adult social care and, in addition, to support the transformation of social care. CSED define reablement as *services for people with poor physical or mental health to help them accommodate their illness by learning or re-learning the skills necessary for daily living* (CSED, 2009a www.csed.dh.gov.uk).

A report on the emerging practice messages for reablement compiled by the SCIE outlined that the focus of a reablement model is on helping to restore independent functioning rather than resolving health care issues, and on helping people to do things for themselves rather than the traditional home care approach of doing things for people that they cannot do for themselves (Social Care Institute for Excellence, (SCIE), 2010).

In addition CSED provide a further definition that reablement is an *approach* or a *philosophy* within home care services – one which aims to help people *do things for themselves*, rather than *having things done for them* (CSED, 2009a, p1).

CASE STUDY

Pauline has been living at home alone for six months since the death of her husband. She has Parkinson's and arthritis and was recently admitted to hospital after fracturing her ankle. She hasn't had any support at home and was feeling very nervous that she might not be able to get in and out of the bath and dress herself once she returned home. The ward staff referred Pauline to the reablement service. Once home she was assessed by an occupational therapist from the reablement team and along with a support worker a programme was implemented that focused on increasing Pauline's confidence in getting in and out of the bath. The support worker visited Pauline every morning and for the first week helped her to get dressed and washed. However, the support worker encouraged Pauline to carry out as much of each task as she could independently and provided verbal support and encouragement.

During the second week the support worker encouraged Pauline to have a bath during her visit. Pauline found getting into the bath very difficult and became quite upset and decided not to carry on with the task. Nevertheless the support worker continued to provide lots of support and encouragement and they discussed the possibility of a bath aid. Pauline felt that she would like to find out more about how a bath aid might work and fit within her bathroom. The occupational therapist visited her again and they agreed on a particular one that they felt would suit Pauline's needs. While Pauline was waiting for the bath aid to arrive and be fitted, the support worker continued to visit and help her with her personal care. The bath aid eventually arrived in the fourth week of Pauline's care package. The support worker visited for a further week and gave her encouragement and guidance on how to use it. By week six, at a review of Pauline's care package with the occupational therapist and support worker, Pauline felt that she now had the confidence to bath herself and no longer required input and support from the reablement service.

The case study highlights the purpose and aims of a reablement service. The approach is different from the more traditional home care service where the focus might be on providing people with care such as washing and dressing them and preparing a meal for them on a regular basis. Reablement is often referred to as a 'hands off' approach with an emphasis on enabling. This approach has led to the need to retrain care staff to enable them to draw upon different skills of care and support such as providing moral support, motivation and encouragement.

In addition, one key feature of a reablement service is the access and implementation of equipment and adaptations such as aids for walking, or grab rails.

ACTIVITY 5.1

Consider some of the potential benefits of reablement services for both the people receiving the service and the economy. What might be some of the negatives of this type of service?

COMMENT

Various studies have been undertaken to identify the benefits and outcomes of reablement services.

In the prospective longitudinal study carried out by CSED (2009a), outcomes for individuals who had received a reablement service were compared with those who had not. The study identified that individuals experienced positive impacts in relation to their health-related quality of life and their social-care-related quality of life up to ten months after reablement.

Furthermore, McLeod and Mair's evaluation of a home care reablement service in Edinburgh identified that the majority of clients interviewed had been discharged from hospital and said they simply would not have been able to cope in the first few weeks after being discharged without the support they had received *(McLeod and Mair, 2009, p35).*

In addition SCIE's report into reablement identified studies that showed that up to 63 per cent of reablement users no longer need the service after six to 12 weeks, and that 26 per cent had a reduced requirement for home care hours *(SCIE, 2010, p3).*

However, the evaluation carried out in Edinburgh identified that some clients of the service had concerns regarding the quality of care received as part of the new package of care delivered at the end of the reablement period, and information about who was going to provide this package of care *(McLeod and Mair, 2009, p36). In addition SCIE highlight, in a paper discussing the emerging practice messages from reablement services, that* results for people with different needs vary. We need to take into account that some people with a high need for assistance will not benefit as much as those with lower support requirements, or may need longer term intensive service *(SCIE, 2010, p3).*

Despite some of these concerns a significant decrease in the need for further social care services has been identified. In addition it was evidenced that costs of reablement were 60 per cent lower than the costs of traditional home care services. This cost did not include the initial service start-up costs (CSED, 2009a).

As a result of this evidence £70 million was allocated to NHS primary care trusts in autumn 2010 to aid the development of reablement services. As a consequence of the government's spending review a further £150 million will be allocated in 2011/12 increasing to £300 million during the years 2012 to 2015 (CSED, 2009a).

This clearly demonstrates the government's commitment to developing reablement services across the country.

ACTIVITY **5.2**

Find out if your local authority provides a reablement service. What is the model used? What is the criterion for accessing the service?

COMMENT

While it is estimated that 88 out of 150 councils are now providing reablement services across England there appears to be no single service model used and there are differences in where the services sit (Joint Improvement Partnership South East 2010).

A prospective longitudinal study carried out in 2009 by CSED identified that some home care reablement services are funded and operated jointly with NHS partners while others are led by adult services departments following reconfiguration of the authorities' home care services.

The study went on to explain that there appear to be two types of service as follows.

- *A discharge service model works with people who have been discharged from hospital. This model is often selective and accepts only people who are certain to benefit from a reablement approach.*

- *An intake service accepts a wide range of people who meet local Fair Access to Care Services (FACS) eligibility criteria and have been referred for home care services (CSED, 2010).*

It appears that most reablement services aim for a six- to 12-week intervention and are therefore time limited.

Intermediate care

Since the implementation of reablement services there has been some confusion caused by the similarity of the service to that of intermediate care. As a social worker, understanding the key differences in these two services will help to support you in accessing the appropriate service. As with reablement there is also no clear model of intermediate care and in some areas reablement sits within the intermediate care function.

In 2009 the Department of Health published updated guidance regarding intermediate care and defined it as:

a range of integrated services to promote faster recovery from illness, prevent unnecessary acute hospital admission and premature admission to long-term residential care, support timely discharge from hospital and maximise independent living.

(DoH, 2009b, p3)

It further identifies that intermediate care is a *function rather than a discrete service* and is *part of a continuum, spanning acute and long-term care, linking with social care reablement* (DoH, 2009b, p10).

Intermediate care appears to focus on prevention of admission to hospital, supporting hospital discharge and helping to prevent or delay admission to long-term residential care. In comparison home care reablement focuses on supporting people to maximise their independence and reduce the need for ongoing home care. Individuals referred to reablement services may have received some form of intermediate care or may be within the community and have not experienced a recent admission to hospital or long-term residential care (CSED, 2009a).

In addition, some of the key differences in the two services lie within eligibility and charging criteria. Intermediate care is not subject to FACS eligibility criteria whereas local authorities decide whether reablement services are subject to FACS or not. For the first six weeks of intermediate care there is no charge; however, this only applies to a reablement service that meets the requirements of the Community Care (Delayed Discharge) Act 2003.

Prior to the Department of Health's updated guidance on intermediate care, people with dementia were often excluded from accessing this type of service. The National Dementia Strategy identified the need for *Improved intermediate care for people with dementia*. This need is now reflected in the updated guidance that suggests that intermediate care teams *need to have competency in mental health and dementia care and ready access to specialists*. It adds that *models of care can involve: recruitment of mental health professionals as core members of a generic intermediate service, to enable members of the team to accept people with dementia or mental health needs with confidence* (DoH, 2009b, p19).

As a result of this guidance, services such as the Mental Health Intermediate Care Service in Nottinghamshire have developed a service which has as its main aims:

- to provide rapid assessment to people in the community who are at risk of losing their independence and to provide support to avoid unnecessary admission to hospital or care;

- to work with individuals and their families to facilitate timely and safe discharge from acute and specialist mental health beds;

- to support people in residential care who wish to return to the community;

- to work with other 'end of life' services to support people to die at home if this is their wish and that of their carers.

One key achievement/benefit of this service has been the improvement in quality of life for people with dementia (DoH, 2011b).

The multidisciplinary approach

In recent years there has been a drive towards professionals with specific expertise working together within one team. These teams are often referred to as multidisciplinary teams. Wilson and Pirrie (2000) note that *one of the main drivers* towards this increased teamworking approach has been the *shift in emphasis from providers of services to a greater focus on client-centredness* (2000, p11). Having access to a number of professionals who sit within the same team can enable the achievement of a *client-centredness* approach. Furthermore a multidisciplinary team can also have financial benefits as the service can be *perceived as one way of ensuring that services are effectively delivered primarily through the avoidance of duplication* (Wilson and Pirrie, 2000, p11).

An example of a multidisciplinary team that people with dementia may benefit from is the Community Mental Health Team (CMHT). Drinkwater (2010) identifies that *social workers and community psychiatric nurses are the mainstay of CMHTs*. He also highlights that other professionals may be part of the team including occupational therapists, psychiatrists and psychologists.

ACTIVITY **5.3**

As Drinkwater suggests, the role of social work is one of the mainstays of a Community Mental Health Team. While benefits have been identified to working within one team with many professionals, what issues might arise as a result of working in this way?

COMMENT

Drinkwater (2010) reflects that there has been an increased number of multidisciplinary teams involving social workers. However, he highlights that social work may not be the predominant profession and practitioners may feel marginalised. Furthermore, he explains that some social workers have expressed concerns that their professional identity could suffer in multidisciplinary teams where other professions take the lead. It will be fundamental for people with dementia that the focus of support doesn't move to one of a purely medical model and that the social needs of the person are not dismissed. Therefore social workers working within a multidisciplinary team should be instrumental in advocating the need to ensure that social needs for people with dementia are considered.

The role of occupational therapy in reablement

In some areas reablement teams have included the role of an occupational therapist (OT). The SCIE visited a few local authorities providing a reablement service and through discussion found that occupational therapy skills were viewed as essential. It was felt, however, that OTs did not necessarily have to be members of the team but their input could help to keep the reablement focus on tasks and aid in training care staff (SCIE, 2010).

The College of Occupational Therapists (COT) states that:

> *the purpose of occupational therapy is to enable people to fulfill, or to work towards fulfilling, their potential as occupational beings. Occupational therapists promote function, quality of life and the realisation of potential in people who are experiencing occupational deprivation, imbalance or alienation. They believe that activity can be an effective medium for remediating dysfunction, facilitating adaptation and recreating identity.*

(COT, 2009, p1).

This statement of purpose appears to fit with the ethos and purpose of a reablement service but furthermore supports the current thinking that people with dementia need to be given the opportunity to fulfil their potential and maintain quality of life.

Davidson and Bissell (2005) argue that *the main thrust of occupational therapy is the philosophy of encompassing wholeness and individuality*. Furthermore they identify that *as occupational therapists we believe that occupation is essential for health and well-being* (2005, pp116–17). SCIE further clarify this approach highlighting that while *reduction in care hours is a key indicator of positive outcomes, it is also important to measure the difference reablement makes to the service user's occupational performance* (SCIE, 2011b, p2). Through access to the Functional Analysis of Care Environments (FACE) and the Canadian Occupational Performance Measure (COPM) tools, occupational therapists are well placed to be able to measure this difference (SCIE, 2011b).

In addition the College of Occupational Therapists argue that *If local authorities want to achieve the best outcomes for both their service users and demonstrable cost benefit for their reablement services they need to involve Occupational Therapists* (College of Occupational Therapists, 2010, p1).

One of the key features of a reablement service involves access to equipment that can support independence; for example, the use of grab rails or trolleys to aid mobility. The knowledge and skills that an OT has regarding appropriate equipment or adaptations is extensive and would clearly add value to a reablement service.

Reablement and people with dementia

Reablement services are open to adults over 18 years old and many local authorities accept all adults. However, a report on an investigation into the longer-term impact of home care reablement services identified that there were *less formal judgements made about the individuals for whom short-term reablement interventions would be appropriate and the level of independence it was considered appropriate to aim for* (Rabiee et al., 2009).

It could be argued that people with dementia are viewed as individuals who might not benefit from reablement services.

ACTIVITY 5.4

What do you think might be some of the barriers for a person with dementia trying to access a reablement service?

COMMENT

It could be argued that because of a lack of understanding and knowledge people with dementia may be excluded from accessing reablement services owing to:

- *a misconception that in order to benefit from a reablement service a person needs to be totally free from intervention after a set period of time;*

- *a belief that all people with dementia have significant memory problems and therefore will not be able to relearn skills;*

- *a perception that there is too much risk in trying to enable someone with dementia to continue to live independently within their own home.*

However, it is heartening to see that there is growing evidence that a number of local authorities are applying an approach based on a social model. These local authorities are selecting people even if it is felt that reablement may only help in achieving small improvements. For example, rather than focusing only on individuals who may achieve total independence following reablement intervention, local authorities are selecting people even if it is felt that reablement may only help in achieving small improvements such as a person being able to make a drink for themselves (Rabiee et al., 2009).

Overcoming the barriers to reablement for people with dementia

It is not about exercise in a chair; it's not about can you get out of that chair yourself but it is about finding out . . . is there any way that we can help you to still get what you want and work around that?

(Manager, quoted in CSED, 2009b, p26)

CASE STUDY

Mrs Links was diagnosed with Alzheimer's disease approximately two years ago. She has continued to live at home without any home care intervention since her diagnosis. Recently she was admitted to hospital following a fall and as a result was referred to the reablement service. Upon her discharge an occupational therapist and reablement support worker visited Mrs Links to establish what support she would require in order to help her regain her lost confidence. An eight-week step-down intervention programme was established and a support worker supported Mrs Links through twice-daily visits. At first Mrs Links required the support worker to take a lead with most tasks. However the support worker quickly encouraged her to undertake tasks such as washing and making meals herself. After four weeks it was identified that Mrs Links now only required a morning visit as she felt confident enough to manage by herself for the rest of the day.

Continued

At the end of the eight weeks and after further discussion with Mrs Links it was felt that ongoing care would be required to support her with her morning routine as she has problems with her cognitive abilities in the morning but these improve over the course of the day.

The Alzheimer's Society response to a consultation on the Personal Care at Home Bill 2010 clearly outlines their support for all people with dementia to be considered for reablement services. However, they also highlight their concern that people with dementia are often excluded from reablement services owing to the view that such services would not be of benefit (Alzheimer's Society, 2010f).

Furthermore the Alzheimer's Society state that any guidance or communication that is produced on reablement needs to discuss the importance of reablement specifically for people with dementia.

RESEARCH SUMMARY

Homecare reablement prospective longitudinal study, interim report 2 of 2, the organisation and content of home care reablement services

In a CSED study carried out in 2009 into reablement services, the way in which such a service can benefit a person with dementia was examined (CSED, 2009b).

The study identified that:

There was a common view among all interviewees that people with dementia and mental health problems required different patterns of engagement, where workers did a wider range of tasks themselves but encouraged clients to help with those tasks. With these clients, reablement work mainly focused on establishing a routine for users, while making sure that the care offered was safe and effective in meeting their needs. Some workers mentioned that they expected much smaller achievements for these groups, such as enabling them to dress themselves, but once clients got a sense of routine, their self-esteem would improve and eventually they would need less long-term support.

(CSED, 2009b, p38)

Conversely, front-line workers thought that reablement was unlikely to produce significant results for service users with dementia or mental health problems, as these people needed continuing support. However, this did not mean that no benefits could be achieved for those groups of service users; rather, that it was much harder to ensure a major improvement in a short period of time. Both managers and workers also felt that reablement was still useful for those groups of people as it could more accurately identify the nature of the long-term support they needed (CSED, 2009b, p46).

In order for a reablement service to benefit people with dementia the approach has to be that the success of the service is based on less care rather than no care.

The contribution of extra care housing

Extra care housing is also referred to as sheltered housing or assisted living and can provide individuals with the opportunity to live independently in a home of their own. The additional benefit of extra care housing is the direct access individuals have to various support services. In some cases properties within an extra care housing service may be used for providing intermediate care or rehabilitation services (Riseborough and Fletcher, 2008).

The National Dementia Strategy identifies the need to consider the potential for extra care housing for people with dementia as stated in objective 10. A scoping review funded by the Joseph Rowntree Foundation identified that *extra care is able to offer some people with dementia an alternative, more independent lifestyle than is possible in a care home (Dutton, 2009, p 4)*. Furthermore, it evidenced that people with dementia living in an extra care housing setting achieved:

> *maximisation of dignity and independence*
>
> *individualised activities and experiences that bring pleasure and a sense of accomplishment (there is some evidence that this may even delay functional decline)*
>
> *effective communication*
>
> *meaningful social interactions*
>
> *ability to maintain meaningful relationships*
>
> *person-centred care*
>
> *freedom from pain and discomfort*
>
> *the ability to age in one place*
>
> *the appropriateness [of the] layout and appearance of the physical environment*
>
> *access to health care and palliative care when needed*
>
> (Dutton, 2009, p5)

While the scoping review outlines the benefits of extra care housing for people with dementia, it also states that *there is strong evidence and general agreement that it is not appropriate for people to enter extra care when they already have advanced dementia* (Dutton, 2009, p5).

ACTIVITY 5.5

Considering the statement above, why might extra care housing be viewed as not being appropriate for people in the later stages of dementia?

COMMENT

The scoping review found that as dementia and/or other conditions worsen, the need for care and support increases and the ability to live independently inevitably diminishes *(Dutton, 2009, p4). However, it could be argued that people with dementia would continue to benefit from extra care housing if the setting is modelled to support only those with dementia and services are available to enable the level of support required.*

CASE STUDY

Extra care scheme for people with specialist needs

The Seven Oaks Dementia Care Unit in Northern Ireland is managed by Fold Housing Association and provides purpose-built specialist extra care. It is designed specifically for people with dementia and provides 30 units, all with en-suite facilities and includes five two-bed bungalows which enable couples to stay together (Care Services Improvement Partnership, 2006).

Assistive technology

Assistive technology has been identified as a key driver to enabling independence for older people. In some local authorities telecare sits within the reablement services with the objective of helping to reduce dependency on longer-term services.

In 2005 the Department of Health identified that telecare offers the promise of enabling thousands of older people to live independently, in control and with dignity for longer (DoH, 2005).

Assistive technology is defined as *any device or system that allows an individual to perform a task that they would otherwise be unable to do, or increases the ease and safety with which the task can be performed* (Royal Commission on Long Term Care, 1999, p325).

ACTIVITY **5.6**

Assistive technology is seen as being able to help to support people with dementia to continue to live in their own home. In what ways can it benefit people with dementia?

COMMENT

There are a number of ways in which assistive technology can help to support and enable people with dementia to live independently. The Alzheimer's Society state that assistive technology and telecare can benefit people with dementia in a number of ways including:

- *promoting independence and autonomy;*

- *helping to manage potential risks in and around the home;*

- *reducing early entry into care homes and hospitals;*

- *facilitating memory and recall;*

- *reducing the stress on carers, improving their quality of life, and that of the person with dementia.*

(Alzheimer's Society, 2011e)

Types of assistive technology

There appear to be two different types of assistive technology. Stand-alone devices are systems that are not linked to a community alarm or monitoring centre and require a person to activate them. In comparison, telecare is a term used to describe equipment such as sensors that are linked to a community alarm or monitoring centre and do not require activation by a person.

The following is an overview of some of the types of assistive technology currently available.

- Personal alarm – a small alarm worn either as a pendant around the neck or strapped to the wrist is linked to a monitoring centre. If a person has fallen or requires support they can activate the alarm and the monitoring centre will respond appropriately.

- Automatic pill dispensers – this acts as a reminder to take medication. The dispenser sounds an alarm at the time of day the medication is needed and an opening in the dispenser enables access to the medication.

- Activity monitor – this device monitors movement within the home. If a person is inactive for a set period of time an alarm is triggered at the monitoring centre and help is called.

- Bed or chair sensor – these sensors alert a monitoring centre when a person has got up from a bed or chair. If the person has not returned after a set period of time, the monitoring centre is alerted.

- Flood detector – this detects water overflow and triggers an alarm at a monitoring centre.

- Magiplug – this device allows a bath or sink to be filled to a certain level. If water rises above this level the device allows it to drain away, reducing the risk of flooding.

- Fall detectors – this can be worn around the neck or wrist and detects impact when a person has previously been standing upright and then falls over. An alarm is then raised at a monitoring centre and help is sent.

- Gas shut-off valve – this device detects gas and shuts off the gas supply. It is helpful for people who sometimes forget to turn off the gas on a cooker.

- Property exit sensors – this will identify if a person has left the property and not returned after a specific period of time. An alarm is triggered at a monitoring centre.

CASE STUDY

Mr Levy has lived alone in his bungalow since the death of his wife three years ago. His son lives 25 miles away and visits him every other weekend. He also has home care support every morning to prompt him to get dressed and support him to prepare his breakfast. However, his son has become increasingly concerned about how Mr Levy is coping during the rest of the day. Upon a recent visit to his father he voiced his concerns and his father agreed that he needed further support. The son was referred to a team who provide information and support on the use of assistive technology. A member of the team visited Mr Levy and his son to discuss their concerns and identify if there were

Continued

any systems or devices that Mr Levy felt would be helpful. During the discussion Mr Levy raised concerns that he had on occasion cooked dinner and forgotten to turn off the gas hob. In addition, he was worried about falling and not being able to get up without help. Following the discussion it was agreed that Mr Levy would try using a gas shut-off valve and a personal alarm. The representative also suggested the use of a smoke detector. The assistive technology enabled Mr Levy to continue to live independently and with no need for further care services at the present time.

Safer walking technology

Safer walking technology is a term used to describe devices that track a person with dementia. There are two types of system, described below.

- An alarm system is used to alert carers when an individual has moved outside a set boundary. It does not enable the individual to be located.

- Tracking devices are used to locate a person at any time or place. (Alzheimer's Society, 2007c)

It has been identified that many people with dementia wish to leave their homes in order to maintain their own independence or to help alleviate boredom. In some cases there are risks associated with a person with dementia leaving their home to walk alone; for example, a person may become lost and forget how to return home.

Tracking devices use satellite technology to track and trace an individual if they have become lost. The person's location can be identified on a computer or mobile phone.

Safer walking technology can assist in providing reassurance to carers and enabling independence for people with dementia.

What benefits are there in the use of assistive technology for people with dementia? What could be some of the negative impacts of using assistive technology for people with dementia?

In addition to enabling a person with dementia to continue to live independently assistive technology can also bring peace of mind for carers and relatives of a person with dementia. However, it is important to remember that assistive technology might not be welcomed by or benefit everybody. Furthermore, people will have differing abilities, needs and preferences and some people may benefit more from care services rather than the use of technology.

AT Dementia, an organisation that provides information on the use of assistive technology for people with dementia notes that assistive technology can encourage loneliness and loss of social contact and should therefore be used as an addition to contact and care (AT Dementia, 2007).

Issues surrounding the use of assistive technology

In a briefing document on safer walking technology the Alzheimer's Society identified ethical concerns regarding its use including concerns that the use of this technology could cause *possible loss of liberty and loss of privacy* (Alzheimer's Society, 2007c, p2). The Society suggests that a balance needs to be struck in order to ensure that a person with dementia is enabled while maintaining their civil liberties and human rights. Furthermore, it recommends that the *opinion of people with dementia should be taken into account when considering the use of technology* and highlights the *importance of seeking the consent of people with dementia* (2007c, p3).

When considering the use of assistive technology AT Dementia provide a set of questions and guidelines to ensure the appropriate use of the technology. In brief the guidelines state the need to identify the following points (AT Dementia, 2007).

- Would the implementation of assistive technology cause more harm than good? For example, does the technology restrict the person with dementia? Or could it have the potential to cause more confusion or distress?

- What are the pros and cons of a particular solution? For example, have the strengths or wishes of the person with dementia been taken into account? Is everyone involved aware of the pros and cons of this technology for the person and their carers?

- What is the purpose of implementing assistive technology? For example, is the technology being used purely to reduce risk or is its purpose to enhance a person's independence? In addition, if the technology is only enabling safety – for example, a door sensor to identify if someone is leaving the house – how is the person with dementia's need being met, i.e. the need to go out?

- Does the situation really need a technological solution? Have other alternatives been looked at? Assistive technology and telecare should not be seen as a 'quick fix'. So it's important to consider what alternatives there might be to using a different approach.

- Has the person with dementia been involved in making a decision about the possible implementation of assistive technology? It is fundamental that we seek the consent of a person with dementia and apply the principles of the Mental Capacity Act 2005 when assessing a person's capacity to make a decision.

Taking these questions into account can help to ensure that assistive technology is used in a positive and enabling way and can help to avoid possible restrictions of privacy and independence (AT Dementia, 2007).

CHAPTER SUMMARY

This chapter has helped to outline the purpose of reablement services and how people with dementia can be empowered through the use of reablement services, extra care housing and assistive technology.

The first part of the chapter provided a definition and purpose of reablement services and considered the different models that are being used. In addition it also examined the benefits of the service, while identifying the similarities to intermediate care. The chapter also explored how people with dementia can

Continued

CHAPTER SUMMARY *continued*

benefit from accessing intermediate care and reablement services. The chapter went on to reflect on the benefits of multidisciplinary working and examined the role of occupational therapy and its value in a reablement service.

The next part of the chapter reviewed how extra care housing can enable independent living for people with dementia while exploring some of the concerns regarding the support of people who are experiencing the later stages of dementia.

Finally the chapter looked at how assistive technology can help to enable independence. The chapter examined the different types of assistive technology and the benefits it can have for people with dementia. The potential issues regarding the use of assistive technology were identified and we looked at guidelines that can support the decision-making process when considering the appropriateness of assistive technology.

FURTHER READING

Marshall, M (2005) *Perspectives on rehabilitation and dementia*. London: Jessica Kingsley Publishers.

This book looks at the issues that have led to people with dementia missing out on physical and psychological rehabilitation. The book demonstrates that rehabilitation has positive outcomes for people with dementia in terms of quality of life and self-esteem.

Dementia Services Development Centre University of Stirling (2010) *Telecare and dementia: Using telecare effectively in the support of people with dementia*. Stirling: University of Stirling.

This book explores how telecare can contribute to the support, protection and quality of life of people with dementia. It also considers the importance of telecare in providing support and reassurance to carers.

Dementia Services Development Centre University of Stirling (2010) *10 Helpful hints for dementia design at home*. Stirling: University of Stirling.

This easy-to-read guide provides simple and practical design solutions to adapt the living environment for people with dementia so that they can live independently for as long as possible. Covering topics such as lighting, interior decor, sound and use of assistive technology, it gives advice on how these elements can be used to their best advantage in the homes of people with dementia.

Department of Health (2009) *Intermediate care – halfway home updated guidance for the NHS and local authorities*. London: DH Publications.

This guidance provides clarification of intermediate care services which changes the way it works in relation to other local services and indicates the way forward for the next few years.

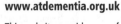

USEFUL WEBSITES

www.atdementia.org.uk

This website provides user-friendly information on assistive technology for people with dementia.

www.housinglin.org.uk

The website of the housing learning and improvement network provides information for meeting the specific needs of people with dementia through housing options.

Chapter 6
The future of dementia care

Introduction

While there has been significant progress in raising the profile of dementia and in developing services and support for both people living with dementia and those caring for them, in a 2010 press release following an interim report into improving dementia services in England the head of the National Audit Office stated that *at the moment this strategy [National Dementia Strategy] lacks the mechanisms needed to bring about large scale improvements and without those mechanisms it is unlikely that the intended and much needed transformation of services will be delivered in the strategy's five year time frame* (National Audit Office, 2010).

Chapter 2 has already identified some of the challenges in implementing the National Dementia Strategy and the government's revised implementation plan prioritising four of the original 17 objectives. This final chapter aims to consider how dementia services need to develop in the future in order to support the needs of people with dementia and achieve the objectives set out in the National Dementia Strategy. In addition, it will consider the role of social work within these services while also providing examples of these developing services.

This chapter will help readers to:

- explore the need to develop early diagnosis and early intervention for people with dementia and the role of memory assessment services within this;

- examine the need to develop services to support carers of people with dementia;

- consider the potential issues relating to hospital stays and the need to improve the hospital discharge process for people with dementia;

- reflect on current community services and how these need to develop to meet the needs of people with dementia;

- be aware of how end of life care is being considered for people with dementia;

- consider the need for training for health and social care professionals to enable development of services.

The £20 billion question

The All-Party Parliamentary Group on Dementia led an inquiry into how lives could be improved through cost-effective dementia services. As a result a report was produced, *The £20 billion question* (2011), which identified that in view of the current financial climate, *we have to ensure money in this area is spent more effectively in supporting people with dementia and their families properly and in a timely way* (All-Party Parliamentary Group on Dementia, 2011, pv). The report suggests eight recommendations for improving support. These include:

1. better collaboration and integration;

2. sharing expertise;

3. early intervention;

4. improved co-ordination;

5. training in dementia care;

6. diagnosis;

7. supporting carers;

8. sharing best practice.

Luengo-Fernandez *et al.*, (2010) state in the Alzheimer's Research Trust *Dementia 2010* report that *every dementia patient costs the economy £27,647 per year: more than UK median salary (£24,700). By contrast, patients with cancer cost £5,999, stroke £4,770 and heart disease £3,455 per year* (Luengo-Fernandez *et al.*, 2010, p5). Yet there is still no clear national care pathway for people with dementia to support them from diagnosis to end of life.

A fundamental outcome of the All-Party Parliamentary Group inquiry was the need to *consider the dementia care system as a whole*. This includes family carers, primary and secondary health care, and social care services (All-Party Parliamentary Group On Dementia, 2011, p9).

ACTIVITY **6.1**

What do you think would be the key benefits for people with dementia, their carers and the economy of considering the dementia care system as a whole?

COMMENT

The inquiry argued that it is important to consider the system as a whole, in order to understand how different areas can best support each other and achieve a better quality, more cost-effective service overall *(All-Party Parliamentary Group, 2011, p9).*

This isn't a new view of how services should be provided. In a reference guide produced by the National Institute for Health and Clinical Excellence (NICE) and the Social Care Institute for Excellence (SCIE) in 2006 the importance of integrated and co-ordinated care is identified. The guidance highlights the need for coordinated delivery of health and social care services *including (NICE, 2006, p22):*

- a combined care plan agreed by health and social services that takes into account the changing needs of the person with dementia and carers;

- named health and social care staff to operate the care plan.

Furthermore, in 2010 NICE issued a Quality standards programme for dementia care *that illustrates measurable quality statements to provide health and social care professionals and people with dementia and their carers a description of high-quality dementia care. Within this document the need for* an integrated approach to provision of services *is also identified and the document argues that this is* fundamental to the delivery of high quality care to people with dementia *(NICE, 2010, p3).*

However, in an interim report into improving dementia services in England in 2010 the National Audit Office highlight that joined-up working remains very patchy and as a result people with dementia are still being unnecessarily admitted to hospital, have longer lengths of stay and enter residential care prematurely *(National Audit Office, 2010, p8).*

The importance of early diagnosis and intervention

The need for early diagnosis and intervention is identified as objective 2 in the National Dementia Strategy. The objective is as follows:

> *Objective 2: Good-quality early diagnosis and intervention for all. All people with dementia to have access to a pathway of care that delivers: a rapid and competent specialist assessment; an accurate diagnosis sensitively communi-*

cated to the person with dementia and their carers; and treatment, care and support provided as needed following diagnosis. The system needs to have the capacity to see all new cases of dementia in the area.

(DoH, 2009a, p33)

However, the All-Party Parliamentary Group argues that *fewer than half of people with dementia receive a diagnosis, meaning there is considerable risk that many people are struggling without the support they need* (All-Party Parliamentary Group on Dementia, 2011, pxii).

Manthorpe and Moriarty (2007) state that it is far too often the case that people with dementia are identified only when they are at crisis point, when a specific incident or carer breakdown highlights the problems the person with dementia is experiencing. Manthorpe and Iliffe (2009, p234) feel that *crises may have been averted if social work support were available earlier*. They explain that *the difficulties of caregivers struggling on unsupported until they become ill themselves may be alleviated by earlier intervention and advice from social workers.*

A recent Department of Health advertising campaign led by the Alzheimer's Society has aimed to increase public awareness of dementia and increase earlier diagnosis.

However, it is estimated that only 31 per cent of people with dementia are registered in GP lists (Luengo-Fernandez, *et al.* 2010). The *Dementia 2010* report, carried out for the Alzheimer's Research Trust, states that *a number of reasons have been proposed for the low rates of diagnosis in primary care settings, including GPs' lack of training and confidence in diagnosing dementia* (Luengo-Fernandez et al., 2010, p26). The All-Party Parliamentary Group on Dementia highlight that *there is some evidence that increasing numbers of GPs consider early diagnosis to be beneficial and are more confident in their ability to recognise dementia*. However, it further highlights that *GPs are very anxious not to get the diagnosis wrong because dementia is such a serious and much-feared condition* (The All-Party Parliamentary Group on Dementia, 2011, p48).

While early diagnosis and intervention has many benefits it could be argued that there is currently a lack of specialist services to support the needs of people with dementia following their diagnosis. In particular, there are concerns regarding the appropriateness of services for younger people diagnosed with dementia. The Royal College of Psychiatrists in a co-published report, *Services for younger people with Alzheimer's disease and other dementias*, highlight that *younger people with dementia and their carers, frequently fall through the net of the health and social care services* (Royal College of Psychiatrists Faculty of Old Age Psychiatry, in conjunction with the Alzheimer's Society, 2005, p5).

CASE STUDY

Linda's husband Paul was diagnosed with Pick's disease, a type of fronto-temporal dementia, when he was 56. Linda and Paul were referred to their local social services department by their GP. A social worker came to visit them to discuss both their needs. Linda didn't feel that she needed support at home and wanted to continue to provide support to Paul

Continued

herself for as long as she could. However, the possibility was discussed that Linda might benefit from some time to herself and the social worker suggested that Paul attend a local day centre once a week. Linda and Paul decided to visit the day centre together. Following their visit, Paul was particularly upset. Although the day centre was warm and friendly, he didn't feel that he wanted to spend the day with people who were much older and at a different stage of the journey through dementia. Unfortunately the couple struggled to find an alternative service that would support the needs of someone younger.

The introduction of memory assessment services

Memory assessment services have been established to meet objective 2 of the National Dementia Strategy. Their primary aim is to diagnose dementia earlier and ensure early intervention. The Department of Health identifies that memory assessment services *should help reduce the risk of crises later in the illness and enable the patient to be cared for at home for as long as possible whilst this is the preferred place of care* (DoH, 2011c, p10). The NICE guide to supporting people with dementia and their carers in health and social care identifies that memory assessment services *should be the single point of referral for people with possible dementia* (NICE, 2006, p12). Furthermore it states that a memory assessment service *should provide*:

> *A responsive service with a full range of assessment, diagnostic, therapeutic and rehabilitation services to accommodate different types and all severities of dementia and the needs of families and carers.*

> *Integrated care in partnership with local health, social care and voluntary organisations.*

> (NICE 2006, p12)

A best practice review produced jointly by the Dementia Services Development Centre and NHS Highland (Szymczynska *et al*., 2010) suggests that memory assessment services *can fulfil a range of functions* including:

- point of referral
- specialist assessment and investigation
- early diagnosis
- education of patient and carer
- counselling of patient and carer
- referral to appropriate agencies

- initiation and monitoring of symptomatic treatments

- advice about the behavioural and psychological symptoms of dementia, and their management

- education of students, postgraduate staff, general practitioners and health planners

(Szymczynska *et al.*, 2010, pp26 and 27)

ACTIVITY **6.2**

Considering the range of functions listed above, which of these would benefit from the skills and input of a social worker?

COMMENT

It is clear that memory assessment services benefit from a multidisciplinary team and would benefit from the skills and input of a social worker. Particular areas that would suit the skills of a social worker could be providing education and counselling/support to people with dementia and their carers. In addition, referral to appropriate agencies suits the role of the social worker. It may well be that even if you are not working as a social worker within a memory assessment service you may be referring individuals to the service.

The following case study illustrates a memory assessment service where, regardless of whether a member of staff has a health or social background, they are trained to provide assessments, diagnosis and treatment.

CASE STUDY

The Croydon Memory Assessment Service

In 2004 a small multidisciplinary team set up a service to aid the early diagnosis of people with dementia. The team, which includes two social workers, work together with the Community Mental Health Team for Older Adults to provide assessments, diagnosis and treatment. This shared responsibility has enabled the service to see greater numbers of people with dementia (Community Care, 2008).

As more memory assessment services develop across the country, Manthorpe and Iliffe (2009) recognise that *social work assessment processes and records may have to include the information that a person is currently undergoing assessment in memory services, rather than recording a diagnosis* (Manthorpe and Iliffe, 2009, p239). Furthermore, it could be argued that more people with dementia may be referred to social services as a result of attending a memory assessment service.

Help and support for carers

Caring for carers: A national strategy for carers (DoH, 1999) was published to support carers who maintain so much of the support and help for potentially vulnerable individuals. The National Dementia Strategy recognised the need to ensure that the provisions of the Carers' Strategy were also made available to carers of people with dementia. Banerjee *et al.*, (2003) identified that people with dementia are 20 times less likely to enter a care home if they are living with and supported by a carer at home. It is therefore fundamental that carers are given the right support and opportunities for respite to enable them to continue with this essential role.

The Alzheimer's Research Trust *Dementia 2010* report (Luengo-Fernandez *et al.*, 2010) evidences that *a total of 1,509 million hours of informal care was provided by friends and relatives of the 517,033 dementia patients living in the community*. In addition it estimates that the total annual cost of informal caregiving is £12,383 million (Luengo-Fernandez, *et al.*, 2010).

The NICE guidance for supporting people with dementia and their carers in health and social care (2006) identifies the need to ensure that *the rights of carers to an assessment of needs as set out in the Carers and Disabled Children Act 2000 and Carers (Equal Opportunities) Act 2004 are upheld*. Furthermore it emphasises that *carers' assessments should seek to identify any psychological distress and the psychosocial impact on the carer, including after the person with dementia has entered residential care* (NICE, 2006, p21).

Manthorpe and Iliffe (2009) argue that *caregivers struggling on unsupported until they become ill themselves may be alleviated by earlier intervention and advice from social workers* (Manthorpe and Iliffe, 2009, p234). Signposting people with dementia and their carers to local support services will be of significant benefit particularly at an early stage.

ACTIVITY *6.3*

Create a resource of the different types of support services that are available for people with dementia in your local area. Having a resource of this nature will be fundamental when supporting and signposting people with dementia and their carers in the community.

COMMENT

Many areas have specific carer support services set up to provide carers with a comfortable, relaxed opportunity to discuss their concerns with other carers who may be experiencing similar circumstances. The following case study highlights an innovative approach to carer support.

Cambridgeshire and Peterborough Dementia Carers' Support Service

The Dementia Carers' Support Service Project is an innovative new service that provides support for carers of people with dementia throughout the journey of their caring role. This is achieved by linking current carers of people with dementia with those who already have first-hand carer experience. These experienced carers become a befriender or buddy and become a Dementia Carers' Support Volunteer (DoH, 2011b).

The role of the dementia adviser

Dementia adviser roles were first suggested in the National Dementia Strategy under *Objective 4: Enabling easy access to care, support and advice following diagnosis*. The Strategy identified the purpose of the role as *a single identifiable point of contact with knowledge and direct access to the whole range of local services available* (DoH, 2009a, p40). It identified that the role of a dementia adviser could be initially to support people with dementia but that this can develop and change to supporting their carers throughout the journey of living with dementia. In order to identify a service model for this new service provision the Department of Health identified that there was a need to *invest in service model development, piloting and evaluation to generate data upon which to make commissioning decisions* (DoH, 2009a, p40). As a result a demonstrator site programme was set up to enable local authorities and health services to submit applications to evidence the benefits or otherwise of dementia adviser services within their local area. Many areas are still developing dementia adviser services and these can vary, with the adviser being based in GP surgeries, hospitals or community mental health teams.

The following case study outlines the role of dementia advisers in Bracknell Forest.

Dementia advisers – Bracknell Forest

Dementia advisers work within and collaboratively with the Joint Community Mental Health Team for Older Adults and the Memory Clinic. They are the identifiable point of contact for people with dementia and their carers and signpost people to appropriate services and enable them to navigate and access support. There are currently 200 people receiving a service from Bracknell Forest Memory Clinic. All people with dementia are able to access the dementia adviser (National Dementia Strategy Demonstrator Sites, 2009a).

The development of peer support networks

To further support people with dementia and their carers the National Dementia Strategy outlined in objective 5 the need for the *Development of structured peer support and learning networks*. There are many examples of peer support groups across other services and each model is different. However, it could be argued that the definition of a peer support group is that it involves *people with an impairment or long-term health condition supporting other people with similar experiences* (Bott, 2008, p6). As with the role of dementia advisers the Department of Health wanted to identify a service model for such peer support for people with dementia and therefore the demonstrator site programme also included the review of peer support networks. The following case study outlines one example of a peer support network submitted to the demonstrator site.

CASE STUDY

The Kent Dementia Peer Support Project

This project is led through a partnership of the local authority, health services and the voluntary sector. The project aimed to utilise web-based technology as well as more traditional meetings and groups to stimulate interaction, support and advice. The main features of the project included:

Social networking – facilitating social networking opportunities via existing Alzheimer's and carers' support organisations and also the Kent dementia website. Establishing a Facebook or Netmums style service where people with dementia and their carers can network virtually with people in a similar situation and/or arrange to meet in large/small groups to share their experiences, concerns and benefit from mutual support.

Information – using the Kent dementia website and Kent TV, the UK's first county council funded on-demand broadband television channel, to offer information, advice and support to people with dementia and their carers. The website will have a dedicated telephone line to provide a listening ear and assist people without web access or who need assistance navigating the website (National Dementia Strategy Demonstrator Sites, 2009b).

Hospital stays and discharge processes for people with dementia

The Alzheimer's Society estimate that up to a quarter of hospital beds are occupied by people with dementia over 65 years of age. In addition it argues that people with dementia stay far longer in hospital than other people who go in for the same procedure. (Alzheimer's Society, 2009). As a result the physical health of people with dementia is impacted and discharge directly to care home is probable. *Hospital care is expensive to provide and hospital stays can have a negative impact upon the symptoms of a person's dementia as well as putting them at risk of complications such as infection and falls* (All-Party Parliamentary Group on Dementia, 2011, p28).

While key issues lie in the care received during the hospital stay, problems with the discharge process are also evident and contribute to people with dementia staying in hospital longer.

ACTIVITY 6.4

What might be some of the issues that contribute to problems with the discharge process for people with dementia?

COMMENT

A report produced by the Older People's Commissioner for Wales Dignified Care? (Older People's Commissioner for Wales, 2011) showed the great difficulty people have in accessing alternative provision for care after a hospital stay, with significantly prolonged stays for those waiting for residential or nursing home care or care packages. Furthermore, a report of the National Audit of Dementia Care in General Hospitals 2011 identified that in half of the case notes reviewed discharge planning had not begun at admission, for no stated reason. It also highlighted that early discharge planning is important to facilitating timely discharge and lessening the time spent by the person with dementia in the acute environment and could also produce savings in cost *(National Audit of Dementia, 2011, p12).*

The Alzheimer's Society has estimated that £80 million could be saved if the length of hospital stays for people with dementia was reduced by one week (Alzheimer's Society, 2009).

CASE STUDY

Darlington Collaborative Acute Care Project

The Darlington Dementia Collaborative has focused on a large-scale change project looking in detail at the admission, assessment, discharge and funding processes related to people with dementia when admitted to a medical elderly care ward in Darlington Memorial Hospital. One of the project's key functions is for improved patient experience through:

- *reduced waiting times for services;*

- *reduced length of stay in hospital;*

- *improved access to specialist services;*

- *improved communication and joint working between services.*

(DoH, 2011b, p56)

However, the All Party-Parliamentary Group on Dementia state that to enable prompt discharge there needs to be further exploration of models of reablement and intermediate care to establish the most effective ways of supporting people with dementia after discharge, and prevent inappropriate readmissions *(All-Party Parliamentary Group on Dementia, 2011, p43).*

The importance of community support services

As previously identified the development of community services to meet the needs of people with dementia is key to ensuring increased quality of life and reduction in hospital admission. There are also significant savings to be made by delaying entry into a care home. The All-Party Parliamentary Group on Dementia suggest that around £72 million can be saved for each month of delay into a care home (All-Party Parliamentary Group on Dementia, 2011).

In previous chapters we have discussed the benefits of the personalisation agenda and reablement services for people with dementia. Key elements of the role of social workers will be understanding these services and their benefits, ensuring they are offered to people with dementia and understanding their contribution towards minimising hospital admission and early entry into a care home.

When considering domiciliary care for people with dementia, social workers will also need to consider its flexibility in meeting the changing and complex needs of people with dementia living in their own homes.

CASE STUDY

Flexible enhanced domiciliary care for people with dementia – Waveney, Suffolk

In Waveney, Suffolk the county council and the local PCT commission a flexible domiciliary care service for people with dementia at times of crisis. This short-term service aims to give an opportunity to stabilise situations and allow for assessment as to people's ongoing needs.

The service is provided by a domiciliary care agency with referrals to it from the older people's mental health social work team.

The All-Party Parliamentary Group on Dementia highlight through their inquiry that a key worker system would contribute to improving the quality and cost-effectiveness of care (All-Party Parliamentary Group on Dementia, 2011, p63). The key worker role would enable one individual to co-ordinate care that would improve the organisation of a care package, enable problems to be spotted and dealt with early on and also reduce the duplication of assessments (All-Party Parliamentary Group on Dementia, 2011, p61).

ACTIVITY *6.5*

While the All-Party Parliamentary Group on Dementia does not state which professional would be suitable in undertaking the role of a key worker, why might this be an appropriate role for a social worker?

Manthorpe and Iliffe (2009, p238) argue that it is social workers who are considered capable of marshalling resources, such as income supplements, to arrange or amend social care support, to liaise with other parts of support system (such as housing, adult safeguarding, transport) and to deal with crises through the exercise of statutory powers or other measures. *Therefore their argument is that* social work may be the discipline with the most desirable characteristics and skills for this role, with its abilities to support people with dementia across a range of services *(p238).*

However, the All-Party Parliamentary Group on Dementia highlight that the role could be taken on by a range of professionals, depending on the individual circumstances of the person with dementia *(All-Party Parliamentary Group on Dementia, 2011, pxiii).*

Improving end of life care

The national end of life care strategy (DoH, 2008c) 'aims to meet the health and social care needs and preferences of all adult patients in where they live and die' (www.endof-lifecareforadults.nhs.uk/publications/eolc-strategy).

In a case note study carried out by Sampson *et al.* (2006) into the care received by people with dementia who died in acute hospitals it was suggested that *patients who are noted to have dementia may be receiving different end-of-life care to those who are cognitively intact* (p188). The study further highlighted that *a large part of good end-of-life care is control of pain, however, pain is poorly managed in patients with dementia* (p188).

The National Dementia Strategy identifies the need to improve this and sets out its plan in objective 12: Improved end of life care for people with dementia. It identifies that people with dementia and their carers need to be involved in planning end of life care and local work on the end of life care strategy needs to be considered.

To further support this objective, the NHS National End of Life Care Programme developed guidance on care towards the end of life for people with dementia (National End of Life Care Programme, 2010). The guidance initially identifies that *the transition for a person with dementia to end of life care will often be difficult* (p5). This is due mainly to the unpredictability of the condition. The guidance emphasises the need for people with dementia to think and plan early for their future care.

Consider the ways in which the role of a social worker may support a person with dementia to plan and discuss their future care.

A social worker may be involved in supporting a person with dementia to access information about advance care planning. Additionally a social worker may be supporting or signposting a person to guidance on making advance decisions and establishing lasting power of attorney. The National End of Life Care Programme (2010) argues that the workforce should be equipped with the skills and confidence to enable open, honest communication about EoLC with individuals and their carers *(p7). It further suggests that* dementia services must up-skill in palliative care issues and palliative care services must up-skill in dementia management *(p8) and* mental health services should appoint a palliative care lead for dementia *(p14) (National End of Life Care Programme, 2010).*

The Peterborough Palliative Care in Dementia Care

This group exists to provide a peer support network for a wide range of professionals in primary and secondary care and the care home sector.

It:

- *provides a local focus for leading on and supporting the implementation of national strategies in relation to palliative care in dementia;*

- *develops and disseminates expertise on working with people with dementia at the end of life, in particular in nursing and residential homes, also in hospital wards and community settings;*

- *sets and improves standards in relation to this;*

- *provides an education and training function through a series of symposia, presentations at conferences, publications and websites.*

(DoH, 2011b)

Better training for supporters of people with dementia

A fundamental underpinning thread to developing and improving services for people with dementia is the need for *an informed and effective workforce for people with dementia* as outlined in objective 13 of the National Dementia Strategy.

To achieve this there is a need for relevant, improved training as previously identified in the NICE guidance to supporting people with dementia and their carers in health and social care. The guidance states that *health and social care managers should ensure all staff working with older people in the health, social care and voluntary sectors have* access to dementia care training (skill development) (NICE, 2006, p24). However, the All-Party Parliamentary Group on Dementia (2011) states that *the level of training amongst health and social care staff is still inadequate . . .* (pxv).

ACTIVITY 6.7

As a social work professional you will be responsible for furthering your knowledge and skills to enable you to support individuals you work with. In what ways can you develop your knowledge and skills in dementia care?

COMMENT

Local authorities are working towards providing varied care training programmes. West Sussex County Council's Learning and Development Department offer training to all staff who are supporting or working with people with dementia. The Social Care Institute for Excellence (SCIE) also provides an e-learning programme and a dementia gateway that showcases best practice in dementia care.

In addition, working alongside other professionals and colleagues will also enable you to develop your knowledge and skills.

CHAPTER SUMMARY

This chapter has explored some of the developing services and areas for people with dementia in support of the National Dementia Strategy. It has considered the impact and benefits of these services, while providing case examples of services already established. The chapter has identified the need for future development in these areas and, furthermore, has examined the role of social work within these services and the importance social work plays in supporting these services.

FURTHER READING

Dementia Services Development Centre (2010) *End of life care for people with dementia: A best practice guide*. Stirling: University of Stirling.

This guide highlights the contribution staff can make in ensuring that the palliative and end of life care of people with dementia fits their needs and preferences. It includes practice examples, practitioner tips, references to research literature, a summary of policy developments and web links.

Andrews, J and House, A (2009) *10 Helpful hints for carers: Practical solutions for carers living with people with dementia*. Stirling: University of Stirling.

This easy-to-read guide for carers living with people with dementia provides simple, practical solutions to the everyday problems family carers can face when looking after a person with dementia. Covering areas like how to cope with aggression, creating relaxing environments, 'wandering', sleeplessness and how to cope with dementia and depression; it is a mine of information and good advice.

Alzheimer's Society and UK Home Care Association *Support and care for people with dementia at home: A guide for homecare workers*. London: Alzheimer's Society.

This guidebook for professionals provides advice, practical tips and strategies on assisting with personal care, protecting the dignity of a person with dementia and helping them remain comfortable and safe.

USEFUL WEBSITES

www.dementiauk.org

This website explains the role of Admiral nurses who are specialist dementia nurses, working in the community, with families, carers and supporters of people with dementia.

www.bettercaring.com

This website provides information for anyone looking for answers about their own care or the care of others.

www.carersuk.org

Carers UK is a charity which aims to improve the lives of carers.

www.dementiaaction.org.uk

This is the website of the the the Dementia Action Alliance. The Alliance is made up of over 80 organisations committed to transforming the quality of life of people living with dementia in the UK and the millions of people who care for them.

www.ncpc.org.uk

This website provides information from the National Council for Palliative Care. They have supported a three-year project on palliative care for people with dementia.

Conclusion

This book has covered a wide range of areas relating to dementia and the role of social work. Through the introduction of the National Dementia Strategy (DoH, 2009a) the need for dementia to be seen as a high priority within health and social care has been identified. As a result it has helped in suggesting key ways of working and best practice approaches for people with dementia. The title of the strategy, *Living well with dementia*, sums up the need to ensure that people with dementia are supported to *live well*, a theme that is explored throughout this book.

The predicated increase in the number of people living with dementia has highlighted that there will inevitably be growing demands on health and social care. This book has taken the opportunity to look at your role as a social worker and how it can aid in empowering people with dementia and support the objectives set within the National Dementia Strategy.

The first chapter of the book provided the opportunity to explore the term dementia and gain an understanding of the most common types of dementia people might be living with. Although it is important within your role to have an awareness of the different types of dementia and possible symptoms a person may experience, the chapter highlights the continuous need to ensure that your practice validates the uniqueness of each individual's personal experience of living with dementia. This has been a key theme of the book and is explored in all chapters of the book.

In supporting the need to view people with dementia as unique individuals a significant part of this chapter looked at how people with dementia can be negatively viewed. The chapter suggested the importance of considering both the medical and the social needs of the person with dementia. In addition it discussed how key professionals have developed models such as Kitwood's Enriched Model of Care (Kitwood, 1997) which provides a framework that encourages the view that people with dementia are people first and foremost.

The chapter provided the opportunity to reflect on Kitwood's suggestion that the experience of living with dementia can be affected by the approach of others. He termed this *social psychology*. The chapter explored in more detail what the term malignant social psychology means and suggested why it might occur within dementia care settings. Furthermore the chapter outlined the potential that tools such as Dementia Care Mapping (DCM) have in observing the lived experience of dementia and the role it can have in identifying malignant social psychology and also in promoting positive person work.

Chapter 1 is instrumental in providing an overview of the experience of dementia and as an introduction to the effects dementia can have for a person with the condition.

To further support the themes explored in Chapter 1, Chapter 2 introduced different government strategies, legislation and guidance that aims to promote positive ways of working with people with dementia and their carers. The chapter argued the need for practitioners to develop an understanding of how government policies can support people with dementia to maintain their independence and autonomy and for the possible need to advocate for and on behalf of people with dementia and their carers. The chapter reviewed some of the objectives of the National Dementia Strategy and suggested that social work has an essential role to play in trying to achieve these objectives. The current issues regarding the implementation of the National Dementia Strategy and the government's decision to publish a revised implementation plan in 2010 were also discussed. The role of social work in the promotion of positive risk-taking for people with dementia was explored and the chapter suggested the need to balance the positive and negatives relating to risk-taking and to move away from a safety first approach to risk. To further support the theme of promoting independence and autonomy for people with dementia the chapter examined the Mental Capacity Act 2005 and considered how this piece of legislation is fundamental in ensuring that people with dementia are provided with a fair framework to support decision-making.

Finally the chapter identified how people with dementia may be at risk of having their human rights violated and suggested the need to develop an understanding of the Human Rights Act 1998 to enable the promotion of the rights of people with dementia. The chapter's overarching theme focuses on the benefits of developing an understanding of and an ability to interpret this legislation and guidance to ensure that people with dementia are treated fairly and are free from discrimination.

In Chapter 3 the role of social work is explored with reference to the issue of safeguarding vulnerable adults. The chapter provided the opportunity to examine definitions and terminology used within safeguarding and identified the importance of key guidance such as *No secrets*. While considering the dilemmas faced in safeguarding vulnerable adults the chapter suggested that people with dementia may have been disempowered due to safeguarding being used in such a way that it influences a person's quality of life. This highlights the benefits of key legislation and policy previously discussed in Chapter 2 that can support social workers to enable and promote well-being and independence for people with dementia.

Furthermore the chapter identified that little research has been carried out on the numbers of people with dementia who experience abuse but suggests that people with dementia may be at greater risk of experiencing abuse. The chapter reflected on the role of social work in developing relationships with care home managers to enable more open relationships and working regarding adults at risk. Moreover it highlighted the importance of developing supportive relationships with carers who may not recognise the impact their behaviour can have on the person with dementia. This chapter highlights how safeguarding people with dementia can ensure that a person is enabled to live well with dementia and is protected from harm. However, a strong theme of the chapter is the need to ensure that people with dementia are not overprotected and therefore at risk of disempowerment.

Acknowledging the introduction of the personalisation agenda, Chapter 4 helped to explore the concept of personalisation and discussed the role of social work in enabling the personalisation of services to become a reality for people with dementia. It suggested that an inadequacy in services led to the need to provide a process that enabled people to have more control about how to meet their own care needs and this has resulted in the personalisation agenda. The chapter discussed how, within social services, self-directed support has been used to enable the implementation of the personalisation agenda and this has seen a move away from traditional care management. It suggested that many people saw personalisation as an opportunity to return to the fundamental elements of social work practice. The chapter argued that for people with dementia there is a greater need for self-directed support in enabling them to have a voice. However, the chapter highlighted that research suggests the uptake of direct payments for people with dementia is low. It suggested a number of reasons for this including that people with dementia and their carers view self-directed support as too complex and time-consuming. The chapter ended by outlining the need for social workers to use their skills in overcoming these issues to ensure that personalisation becomes a reality for people with dementia.

While Chapter 4 shows how self-directed support promotes the ability of people with dementia to assess and determine their own care needs, Chapter 5 helps to explore how independence can be enabled for people with dementia through services such as reablement, intermediate care, extra care housing and assistive technology. The chapter provided clarity regarding the similarities between reablement and intermediate care and reflected on the benefits both for people receiving a reablement service and in terms of the potential savings for the economy. It suggested the role social work might have in advocating the social needs of people with dementia while working within multidisciplinary teams such as Community Mental Health Teams. In addition the chapter identified the benefits occupational therapy can have within a reablement service. However, the chapter suggested potential barriers for people with dementia accessing reablement services and suggested the need for a reablement service to develop an approach where the success of the service is based on less care rather than no care. The chapter explored additional ways of enabling people to live more independently and examined the benefits of extra care housing while suggesting the need for specialist extra care housing schemes to meet the needs of people who are in the later experiences of dementia. Assistive technology was also examined and different types of technology were explored. However, the chapter is mindful of the potential ethical issues linked to the use of assistive technology and provided guidelines that promote consideration of both the benefits and the issues to explore when considering the use of assistive technology. This chapter helps to challenge the view that people with dementia cannot be enabled to continue to live independently in their own homes.

These chapters have highlighted key legislation and policy and identified developing services that can promote well-being, autonomy and independence for people with dementia, Chapter 6 considered how services need to continue to develop in order to fully support the needs of people with dementia and to make the National Dementia Strategy a reality. This final chapter explored the development of services for people with dementia and considered the role of social work within these services. However, it argued the need for health and social care to develop integrated approaches for people with dementia to ensure that they receive a seamless and cost-effective service. The chapter provided various examples of innovative services for people with dementia and discussed the role of social work within these services.

There is still much to learn regarding the support of people with dementia. The implementation of the National Dementia Strategy has seen a significant step towards ensuring that people with dementia are given a voice. It is imperative that we continue to listen to what people with dementia want and involve them in the design and delivery of services. In your role as a social worker you will be fundamental in taking this forward and advocating for people with dementia to ensure that their voices continue to be heard.

Appendix 1 Professional capabilities framework

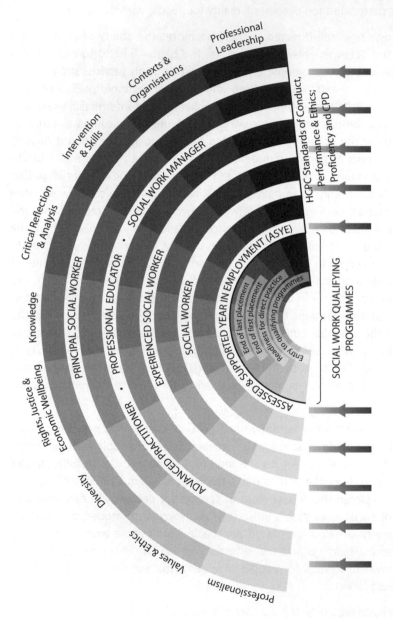

Professional Capabilities Framework diagram reproduced with permission of The College of Social Work.

Appendix 2 Subject benchmark for social work

Subject knowledge, understanding and skills

Subject knowledge and understanding

5.1 During their degree studies in social work, honours graduates should acquire, critically evaluate, apply and integrate knowledge and understanding in the following core areas of study.

5.1.1

Social work services, service users and carers, which include:

- the social processes (associated with, for example, poverty, migration, unemployment, poor health, disablement, lack of education and other sources of disadvantage) that lead to marginalisation, isolation and exclusion, and their impact on the demand for social work services;

- explanations of the links between definitional processes contributing to social differences (for example, social class, gender, ethnic differences, age, sexuality and religious belief) to the problems of inequality and differential need faced by service users;

- the nature of social work services in a diverse society (with particular reference to concepts such as prejudice, interpersonal, institutional and structural discrimination, empowerment and anti-discriminatory practices);

- the nature and validity of different definitions of, and explanations for, the characteristics and circumstances of service users and the services required by them, drawing on knowledge from research, practice experience, and from service users and carers;

- the focus on outcomes, such as promoting the well-being of young people and their families, and promoting dignity, choice and independence for adults receiving services;

- the relationship between agency policies, legal requirements and professional boundaries in shaping the nature of services provided in interdisciplinary contexts and the issues associated with working across professional boundaries and within different disciplinary groups.

5.1.2

The service delivery context, which includes:

- the location of contemporary social work within historical, comparative and global perspectives, including European and international contexts;

- the changing demography and cultures of communities in which social workers will be practising;

- the complex relationships between public, social and political philosophies, policies and priorities and the organisation and practice of social work, including the contested nature of these;

- the issues and trends in modern public and social policy and their relationship to contemporary practice and service delivery in social work;

- the significance of legislative and legal frameworks and service delivery standards (including the nature of legal authority, the application of legislation in practice, statutory accountability and tensions between statute, policy and practice);

- the current range and appropriateness of statutory, voluntary and private agencies providing community-based, day-care, residential and other services and the organisational systems inherent within these;

- the significance of interrelationships with other related services, including housing, health, income maintenance and criminal justice (where not an integral social service);

- the contribution of different approaches to management, leadership and quality in public and independent human services;

- the development of personalised services, individual budgets and direct payments;

- the implications of modern information and communications technology (ICT) for both the provision and receipt of services.

5.1.3

Values and ethics, which include:

- the nature, historical evolution and application of social work values;

- the moral concepts of rights, responsibility, freedom, authority and power inherent in the practice of social workers as moral and statutory agents;

- the complex relationships between justice, care and control in social welfare and the practical and ethical implications of these, including roles as statutory agents and in upholding the law in respect of discrimination;

- aspects of philosophical ethics relevant to the understanding and resolution of value dilemmas and conflicts in both interpersonal and professional contexts;

- the conceptual links between codes defining ethical practice, the regulation of professional conduct and the management of potential conflicts generated by the codes held by different professional groups.

5.1.5

The nature of social work practice, which includes:

- the characteristics of practice in a range of community-based and organisational settings within statutory, voluntary and private sectors, and the factors influencing changes and developments in practice within these contexts;

- the nature and characteristics of skills associated with effective practice, both direct and indirect, with a range of service users and in a variety of settings;

- the processes that facilitate and support service user choice and independence;

- the factors and processes that facilitate effective interdisciplinary, interprofessional and interagency collaboration and partnership;

- the place of theoretical perspectives and evidence from international research in assessment and decision-making processes in social work practice;

- the integration of theoretical perspectives and evidence from international research into the design and implementation of effective social work intervention, with a wide range of service users, carers and others;

- the processes of reflection and evaluation, including familiarity with the range of approaches for evaluating service and welfare outcomes, and their significance for the development of practice and the practitioner.

Appendix 3
Useful contacts

The Alzheimer's Society

The Alzheimer's Society works to improve the quality of life of people affected by dementia in England, Wales and Northern Ireland.

Devon House, 58 St Katharine's Way, London E1W 1JX
Phone: 020 7423 3500
E-mail: enquiries@alzheimers.org.uk
Website: www.alzheimers.org.uk/

Alzheimer Scotland

Alzheimer Scotland provides a wide range of services for people with dementia and their carers.

22 Drumsheugh Gardens, Edinburgh EH3 7RN
Phone: 0131 243 1453
E-mail: alzheimer@alzscot.org
Website: www.alzscot.org.uk

Alzheimer's Research UK (Formerly the Alzheimer's Research Trust)

This is the UK's leading dementia research charity specialising in finding preventions, causes, treatments and a cure for dementia.

The Stables, Station Road, Great Shelford, Cambridge CB22 5LR
Phone: 01223 843899
E-mail: enquiries@alzheimers-research.org.uk
Website: www.alzheimers-research.org.uk

The Association for Dementia Studies, University of Worcester

This is a multiprofessional group of educationalists, researchers and practitioners who are expert in the field of person-centred dementia care and support.

Institute of Health and Society, St John's Campus, University of Worcester, Worcester WR2 6AJ
Phone: 01905 855250
E-mail: dementia@worc.ac.uk
Website: ihsc.worc.ac.uk/dementia

DASN International

This is an Internet-based support network organised by and for people with dementia.
Website: www.dasninternational.org

The Pick's Disease Support Group

The group aims to support people with fronto-temporal dementia and their carers.

8 Brooksby Close, Oadby, Leicester LE2 5AB
Phone: 0116 271 1414
E-mail: info@pdsg.org.uk
Website: www.pdsg.org.uk

The Lewy Body Society

The Lewy Body Society, is the only charity in Europe exclusively concerned with Dementia with Lewy bodies. The charity's mission is to raise awareness of DLB for the general public and educate those in the medical profession.

E-mail: info@lewybody.org
Website: www.lewybody.org

Young Dementia UK

This is a service based in Oxfordshire for younger people with dementia.

PO Box 315, Witney, Oxfordshire OX28 1ZN
Phone: 01993 776295
E-mail: mail@youngdementiauk.org
Website: www.youngdementiauk.org

Dementia UK

This UK charity developed and supports the role of Admiral Nurses.

6 Camden High Street, London, NW1 0JH
Phone: 020 7874 7210
E-mail: info@dementiauk.org
Website: www.dementiauk.org

Age UK

Astral House, 1268 London Road, London SW16 4ER
Phone: 020 8765 7200
E-mail: contact@ageuk.org.uk

Skills for Care

West Gate, 6 Grace Street, Leeds, LS1 2RP
Phone: 0113 245 1716
E-mail: info@skillsforcare.org.uk

Glossary

Acetylcholinesterase inhibitors A group of drugs that can help slow the progression of some of the symptoms of Alzheimer's disease.

Admiral nurse These individuals specialise in working with people with dementia and their carers. They can provide information, practical advice, and help other professionals to deliver positive care. Admiral Nurses Direct is an advice and support line which can be called on 0845 257 9406 or e-mailed on direct@dementiauk.org.

Advanced care planning This term covers a number of processes that enable people who currently have capacity the opportunity to make preparations for a time when they may lack capacity.

Alzheimer's disease The commonest cause of dementia. Common symptoms include difficulties with short-term memory and with undertaking everyday tasks. First described by a German doctor, Alois Alzheimer.

Alzheimer's Research UK Alzheimer's Research UK is the UK's leading dementia research charity.

Alzheimer's Society Alzheimer's Society is a membership organisation which works to improve the quality of life of people affected by dementia in England, Wales and Northern Ireland.

Amyloidal plaques A term for protein fragments that the body produces normally.

Anti-dementia medication A group of medicines prescribed to slow the progression of some of the symptoms of Alzheimer's disease.

Antipsychotic medication A group of drugs produced to treat conditions that cause a person to experience psychosis, i.e. seeing and/or hearing things that are not real or true.

Assistive technology A term that includes assistive, adaptive and rehabilitative devices to enable people to achieve independent living.

Association of Directors of Adult Social Services (ADASS) The Association of Directors of Adult Social Services (ADASS) represents all the directors of adult social services in England.

Binswanger's disease This is a type of dementia caused by widespread, microscopic areas of damage to the deep layers of white matter in the brain.

Canadian occupational performance measure (COPM) This is an outcome measure designed for occupational therapists.

Care Quality Commission (CQC) The CQC regulates, inspects and reviews all adult health and social care services in the public, private and voluntary sectors in England.

Care services efficiency delivery (CSED) The CSED helps local authorities to develop more efficient ways of delivering adult social care.

College of Occupational Therapists The college sets professional and educational standards for the occupational therapy profession.

Creutzfeldt-Jakob disease (CJD) This is a disease of the nervous system that causes damage to the brain.

Dementia This is an umbrella term used to describe a group of symptoms that can be caused by different conditions affecting a person's brain.

Dementia Action Alliance The Alliance is made up of over 80 organisations in the UK who have signed up to a National Dementia Declaration to try and improve services for people with dementia.

Dementia Care Mapping (DCM) An observational tool developed by the late Professor Tom Kitwood.

Dementia UK A report commissioned by the Alzheimer's Society that explored the prevalence and economic cost of dementia. This is also the name of a national charity.

Dementia with Lewy Bodies A type of dementia that shares similar characteristics to both Parkinson's and Alzheimer's disease.

Deprivation of Liberty Safeguards A set of safeguards designed to protect the liberty of individuals.

Direct payment This is a cash payment that comes from the local authority to a person who has agreed to receive their budget in this way and is able to make arrangements to have their social care needs met. If a person is not able to give their agreement to receiving a direct payment then a suitable person can be chosen to act on behalf of that individual.

Enriched model Professor Tom Kitwood's equation to illustrate the many factors that can influence a person's experience of dementia.

Fair Access to Care Services (FACS) provides local authorities with guidance on eligibility criteria for adult social care.

Fronto-temporal dementia This is a term used to cover a range of conditions such as Pick's disease.

Functional Analysis of Care Environments (FACE) Is an assessment tool designed for adults' and older people's mental health settings.

Health Economics Research Centre The centre carries out research on the economic aspects of health and disease.

Intermediate care A type of service that supports people in their own homes to maintain or regain independence.

Joint Improvement Partnership South East The Joint Improvement Partnership leads and guides the improvement of adult social care in the south-east.

Judicial review A judicial review is a type of court proceedings whereby a judge reviews decisions or actions made by a public body.

Korsakoff's syndrome A disorder of the brain usually associated with heavy alcohol consumption over a long period.

Local Government Association (LGA) An organisation that aims to achieve a common cross-party position on issues.

Malignant social psychology A term psychologist Tom Kitwood used to describe poor interaction and communication with people with dementia.

Medical model of dementia This theory of dementia concentrates on what is physically happening in the brain as a consequence of having dementia.

Mini mental state examination A test used to assess a person's cognitive ability.

Motor neurone disease A progressive neurodegenerative disease.

Multidisciplinary team A team of various different professionals working together to provide a holistic approach for individuals.

National Dementia Strategy This is the Department of Health's five-year strategy outlining its plans for improving health and social care services for people with dementia and their carers.

National Institute of Health and Clinical Excellence (NICE) NICE provide evidence-based guidance on effective ways to prevent, diagnose and treat disease and ill health.

Neurofibrillary tangles These are insoluble twisted fibres found inside the brain's cells and consist mainly of a protein called **tau.**

Non-pharmacological Refers to therapy that does not involve the use of medication.

No secrets This was guidance produced by the Department of Health on developing and implementing multi-agency policies and procedures to protect vulnerable adults from abuse.

Parkinson's disease A degenerative neurological disorder.

Personal budget A pot of money that is given to a person who is eligible for adult social care, to use to purchase services that will meet their social care needs.

Personal Care at Home Bill Announced in 2009 the bill will provide free personal care at home to those who have the greatest need.

Personalisation agenda A term used to describe the reforms being made in health and social care to focus on and be led by the individuals who use a service.

Pick's disease This type of dementia initially affects the front part of a person's brain, known as the frontal lobe. Later it goes on to affect a part of the brain called the temporal lobe. This part of the brain is involved in memory.

Prevalence rates A way of identifying the number of people within a population who have a disease at a given time.

Proportionality A term relating to the Human Rights Act 1998. Public authorities have to protect a person's rights in a way that is appropriate and not excessive.

Psychological therapy A therapy that involves talking through problems with a trained therapist.

Reablement Services are for people with poor physical or mental health to help them accommodate their illness by learning or relearning the skills necessary for daily living (Care Services Efficiency Delivery Programme (CSED, 2009).

Royal College of Psychiatrists The professional and educational body for psychiatrists.

Self-directed support The overall system that is used by local authorities to give people who are eligible for support control over how they use the money given to them to meet their social care needs.

Social Care Institute for Excellence (SCIE) Provides guidance and shares knowledge about what works within social care.

Social model of dementia This theory of dementia concentrates on how the experience of dementia is affected by other people in society and the environment in which the person with dementia lives.

Support plan A plan that is developed and produced by an individual (with support if needed) which describes how they are going to use their personal budget to meet their social care needs.

Telecare A service that helps people to live independently in their own homes. Telecare provides equipment and devices to enable this to happen.

Vascular dementia Is caused by oxygen failing to reach brain cells as a result of problems with blood supply (the vascular system).

Vascular system The network of veins and arteries that carries blood around the body.

Vulnerable adult *An adult aged 18 years or over who is or may be in need of community care services by reason of mental or other disability, age or illness; and who is or may be unable to take care of him or herself, or unable to protect him or herself against significant harm or exploitation* (Lord Chancellor's Department, 1997).

References

Action against Elder Abuse (2011) *A critical analysis of the CQC dignity and nutrition inspections of 100 hospitals in England*. London: Action against Elder Abuse.

ADASS (2005) *Safeguarding adults: A national framework of standards for good practice and outcomes in adult protection work*. London: ADASS.

ADASS (2009) *Making progress with putting people first: Self-directed support*. London: DH/ADASS.

Aguirre, E, Spector, A, Hoe, J, Russell, IT, Knapp, M, Woods, RT and Orrell, M (2010) Maintenance cognitive stimulation therapy (CST) for dementia: A single-blind, multi-centre, randomized controlled trial of Maintenance CST vs. CST for dementia. *Trials*, 11 (46).

Allan, K and Killick, J (2000) Undiminished possibility: The arts in dementia care. *Journal of Dementia Care*, 8 (3), 16–18.

Allen, K and Glasby, J (2010) 'The billion dollar question': Embedding prevention in older people's services – 10 'high impact' changes. Health Services Management Centre. Discussion paper, University of Birmingham. Birmingham: University of Birmingham.

All-Party Parliamentary Group on Dementia (2008) *Always a last resort: Inquiry into the prescription of antipsychotic drugs to people with dementia living in care homes*. London: House of Commons.

All-Party Parliamentary Group on Dementia (2010) *A misspent opportunity? Inquiry into the funding of the National Dementia Strategy*. London: House of Commons.

All-Party Parliamentary Group on Dementia (2011) *The £20 billion question: An inquiry into improving lives through cost-effective dementia services*. London: House of Commons.

Alzheimer Scotland Action on Dementia (2002) *Vascular Dementia Information Sheet*. Edinburgh: Alzheimer Scotland.

Alzheimer's Society (2002) *Is free nursing care 'unfair and unworkable?.'* London: Alzheimer's Society.

Alzheimer's Society (2007a) *Dementia UK: A report to the Alzheimer's Society on the prevalence and economic cost of dementia in the UK produced by King's College London and London School of Economics*. London: Alzheimer's Society.

Alzheimer's Society (2007b) *A home from home: A report highlighting opportunities for improving standards of dementia care in care homes*. London: Alzheimer's Society.

Alzheimer's Society (2007c) *Safer walking technology*. London: Alzheimer's Society.

Alzheimer's Society (2009) *Counting the cost: Caring for people with dementia on hospital wards*. London: Alzheimer's Society.

Alzheimer's Society (2010a) *What is dementia with Lewy bodies? Factsheet 403*. London: Alzheimer's Society.

Alzheimer's Society (2010b) *What is fronto-temporal dementia (including Pick's disease)? Factsheet 404*. London: Alzheimer's Society.

Alzheimer' Society (2010c) *What is Korsakoff's syndrome? Factsheet 438*. London: Alzheimer's Society.

Alzheimer's Society (2010d) *What is Creutzfeldt-Jakob disease (CJD)? Factsheet 427*. London: Alzheimer's Society.

Alzheimer's Society (2010e) *People with dementia living alone*. London: Alzheimer's Society.

Alzheimer's Society (2010f) *Alzheimer's Society Response to the Department of Health Personal Care at Home Consultation on Regulations and Guidance*. London: Alzheimer's Society.

Alzheimer's Society (2011a) *What is Alzheimer's Disease? Factsheet 402*. London: Alzheimer's Society.

Alzheimer's Society (2011b) *Drug treatments for Alzheimer's disease*. Factsheet 407. London: Alzheimer's Society.

Alzheimer's Society (2011c) *Care and support of people with dementia in their own homes*. London: Alzheimer's Society.

Alzheimer's Society (2011d) *Short changed: Protecting people with dementia from financial abuse*. London: Alzheimer's Society.

Alzheimer's Society (2011e) *Assistive technology – devices to help with everyday living*, Factsheet 437, London: Alzheimer's Society.

Anetzberger, G, Palmisano, B, Sander, M, Bass, D, Dayton, C, Eckert, S and Schimer, M (2000) A model intervention for elder abuse and dementia. *The Gerontologist*, 40 (4), 492–7.

Archibald, C (2006) Meeting the nutritional needs of patients with dementia in hospital. *Nursing Standard*, 20, 41–5.

AT Dementia (2007) Available online at www.atdementia.org.uk/editorial.asp?page_id=25 (accessed April 2012).

Baker, R, Holloway, J, Holtkamp, CCM, Larsson, A, Hartman, LC, Pearce, R, Scherman, B, Johansson, S, Thomas, P, Wareing, L and Owens, M (2003) Effects of multi-sensory stimulation for people with dementia. *Journal of Advanced Nursing*, 43 (5), 465–77.

Banerjee, S (2009) *The use of antipsychotic medication for people with dementia: Time for action*. London: The Stationery Office.

Banerjee, S, Murray, J, Foley, B, Atkins, L. Schneider, J. Mann, A (2003) Predictors of institutionalisation in people with dementia. *Journal of Neurology, Neurosurgery and Psychiatry*, 74 (9), 1315–16.

BBC *Panorama* (2011) Available at: www.news.bbc.co.uk/programmes/6011pwt6# programme-broadcasts (accessed April 2012).

Boniface, S (2009) Gran, 91, left to die in agony in care home. *Daily Mirror*, 10 May.

Bott, S (2008) *Review of peer support activity in context of self-directed support and the personalisation of adult social care*. London: National Centre for Independent Living.

Bourn, *et al*. (2007) *Improving services and support for people with dementia*. London: National Audit Office.

Boyle, G (2008) The Mental Capacity Act 2005. Promoting the citizenship of people with dementia? *Health and social care in the community*, 16 (5), 529–37.

British Association of Social Workers (2002) The code of ethics for social work. *British Journal of Clinical Psychology*, 43, 177–96.

Brodaty, H, Thompson, C and Fine, M (2005) Why caregivers of people with dementia and memory loss don't use services. *International Journal of Geriatric Psychiatry*, 20 (6), 537–46.

Brooke, C (2010) Care home staff tormented dementia victims and recorded their 'despicable' acts on their mobile phones. *Daily Mail*, 15 December.

Brooker, D (2007) *Person-centred dementia care: Making services better*. London: Jessica Kingsley Publishers.

Brooker, D and Surr, C (2005) *Dementia care mapping: Principles and practice*. Bradford: Bradford Dementia Studies.

Bruce, E and Austin, M (2000) Social work supervision: Assessing the past and mapping the future. *The Clinical Supervisor*, 19 (2), 85–107.

Burrow, E (2009) Direct payments and older people: Developing a framework for practice. In Gaplin, D and Bates, N (eds) *Social work practice with adults*. Exeter: Learning Matters.

Buttell, P (1999) The relationship between spouse abuse and the maltreatment of dementia sufferers. *American Journal of Alzheimer's Disease*, 14 (4), 230–32.

Care Council for Wales (2010) *Care at home: Challenges, possibilities and implications for the workforce in Wales*. Cardiff: Care Council for Wales.

Care Quality Commission (2010) *The adult social care market and the quality of services*. London: Care Quality Commission.

Care Services Efficiency Delivery Programme (CSED) (2009a) *Homecare reablement prospective longitudinal study, interim report 1 of 2, the short-term outcomes and costs of reablement services*. London: DH Publications.

Care Services Efficiency Delivery Programme (CSED) (2009b) *Homecare reablement prospective longitudinal study, interim report 2 of 2, the organisation and content of home care reablement services*. London: DH Publications, 38, 46.

Care Services Efficiency Delivery Programme (CSED) (2009c) *Homecare reablement toolkit, intermediate care and homecare reablement: What's in a name?* London: DH Publications.

Care Services Efficiency Delivery Programme (CSED) (2010) *Homecare reablement prospective longitudinal study final report summary*. London: DH Publications.

Care Services Improvement Partnership (2006) *The extra care housing toolkit*. London: Care Services Improvement Partnership.

Carr, S (2010) *Personalisation: A rough guide*. London: Social Care Institute for Excellence.

Carruthers, I and Ormondroyd, J (2009) *Age equality in health and social care*. London. The Stationery Office.

Chamber's Dictionary (2008) *The Chambers Dictionary* (11th edition). Edinburgh: Chambers Harrap Publishers Ltd.

Chan, P and Chan, T (2009) The impact of discrimination against older people with dementia and its impact on student nurses' professional socialization. *Nurse Education in Practice*, 9 (4), 221–7.

Clare, L (2004) Awareness in early stage Alzheimer's disease: A review of methods and evidence. *British Journal of Clinical Psychology*, 43, 177–96.

Coaten, R (2001) Exploring reminiscence through dance and movement. *Journal of Dementia Care*, 9 (5), 19–22.

College of Occupational Therapists (2009) *Curriculum guidance for pre-registration Education*. London: College of Occupational Therapists.

College of Occupational Therapists (2010) *Position statement reablement: The added value of occupational therapists*. London: College of Occupational Therapists.

Commission for Social Care Inspection (CSCI) (2006) *Time to care*. London: Care Quality Commission.

Community Care (2008) Croydon leads on dementia. *Community Care*, 31 July.

Cooper, C, Selwood, A, Blanchard, M, Walker, Z, Blizard, R and Livingston, G (2009) Abuse of people with dementia by family carers: Representative cross sectional survey. *British Medical Journal*, 338, 155–7.

Cooper, C, Selwood, A and Blanchard, M (2010) Abusive behaviour experienced by family carers from people with dementia: The CARD (caring for relatives with dementia) study. *Journal of Neurology, Neurosurgery, and Psychiatry*, 81, 592–6.

Cox, S and Keady, J (1999) *Younger people with dementia: Planning, practice and development*. London: Jessica Kingsley Publishers.

Coyne, A, Reichman, W and Berbig, L (1993) The relationship between dementia and elder abuse. *American Journal of Psychiatry*, 150, 643–6.

CSCI (2008a) *See me, not just the dementia: Understanding people's experiences of living in a care home*. London: CSCI.

CSCI (2008b) *State of social care in England 2006–7*, London: CSCI.

Daily Mail (2009) Available at: www.dailymail.co.uk/femail/article-1173325/I-numb-I-Daughter-blasts-Gestapo-social-services-bundle-mother-86-family-home.html (accessed April 2012).

Daily Telegraph (2009) Available at: www.telegraph.co.uk/health/elderhealth/5221132/ Daughter-of-dementia-sufferer-says-Its-my-mums-right-to-live-and-die-with-her-family.html (accessed April 2012).

Davidson, C and Bissell, R (2005) In Marshall, M (ed.) *Perspectives on rehabilitation and dementia*. London: Jessica Kingsley Publishers, 116–117.

Dean, R, Proudfoot, R and Lindesay, J (1993) The quality of interactions schedule (QUIS): Development, reliability and use in the evaluation of two domus units. *International Journal of Geriatric Psychology*, 8 (10), 819–26.

Deighton, T (2009) Staffordshire hospital scandal: The hidden story. *Daily Telegraph*, 22 March.

Department for Constitutional Affairs (2007) *Mental Capacity Act 2005 Code of Practice*. London: The Stationery Office.

Department of Health (DoH) (1999) *Caring for carers: A national strategy for carers*. London: DH Publications.

Department of Health (2003) *Direct payments guidance: Community care, services for carers and children's services (direct payments) guidance England 2003*. London: Department of Health.

Department of Health (2005) *Building telecare in England*. London: DH Publications.

Department of Health (DoH) (2006) *Our health, our care, our say: A new direction for community services*. London: DoH Publications.

Department of Health (2008a) *Consultation on the review of the no secrets guidance: Invitation to the local safeguarding partnerships*. London: The Stationery Office.

Department of Health (2008b) *Safeguarding adults: A consultation on the review of the 'no secrets' guidance*. London: The Stationery Office.

Department of Health (DoH) (2008c) *End of life care strategy. Promoting high quality care for all adults at the end of life*. London: DH Publications.

Department of Health (DoH) (2009a) *Living well with dementia: A national dementia strategy*. London: DoH Publications.

Department of Health (DoH) (2009b) *Intermediate care – halfway home updated guidance for the NHS and local authorities*. London: DoH Publications.

Department of Health (DoH) (2009c) *Safeguarding adults: Report on the consultation on the review of 'No secrets'*. London: DoH Publications.

Department of Health (2009d) *Living well with dementia: A national dementia strategy: Demonstrator site programme*. London: Department of Health.

Department of Health (DoH) (2010a) *NHS support for social care: 2010/11–2012/13*. London: DoH Publications.

Department of Health (DoH) (2010b) *Quality outcomes for people with dementia: Building on the work of the national dementia strategy*. London: DoH Publications.

Department of Health (2010c) *Nothing ventured, nothing gained: Risk guidance for people with dementia*. London: Department of Health.

Department of Health (2010d) *Recognised, valued and supported: Next steps for the carers' strategy*. London: Department of Health.

Department of Health (2011a) *Statement of government policy on adult safeguarding*. London: The Stationery Office.

Department of Health (2011b) *Living well with dementia: A national dementia strategy: good practice compendium – an assets approach*. London: Department of Health.

Department of Health (DoH) (2011c) *Service specification for dementia: Memory service for early diagnosis and intervention*. London: DoH Publications.

Department of Health and Care Services Improvement Partnership (2005) *Everybody's business. Integrated mental health services for older adults: A service development guide*. London: Department of Health.

Department of Health and Home Office (2000) *No secrets: Guidance on developing and implementing multi-agency policies and procedures to protect vulnerable adults from abuse*. London: The Stationery Office.

Drinkwater, M (2010) *Working in teams and joint working*. London: *Community Care*, available at: www.communitycare.co.uk/Articles/09/12/2010/108595/Multidisciplinary-teams.htm (accessed April 2012).

Dutton, R (2009) *'Extra care' housing and people with dementia: A scoping review of the literature 1998–2008*. Housing and Dementia Research Consortium.

Equality and Human Rights Commission (2011) *Close to home: An inquiry into older people and human rights in home care*. London: Equality and Human Rights Commission.

Gaugler, JE, Kane, RL, Kane, RA and Newcomer, R (2005) Early community-based service utilization and its effects on institutionalization in dementia caregiving. *The Gerontologist*, 45, 177–85.

Hansberry, M, Chen, E and Gorbien, M (2005) Dementia and elder abuse. *Clinics in Geriatric Medicine*, 21 (2), 315–32.

HM Government (2007) *Putting people first: A shared vision and commitment to the transformation of adult social care*. London: the Stationery Office.

HM Government (2008) *Carers at the heart of 21st century families and communities: A caring system on your side, a life of your own*. London: HM Government.

Home Office (2006) *Keep safe: A guide to personal safety*. London: Home Office.

Individual Budgets Evaluation Network (2008) *Evaluation of the individual budgets pilot programme: Final report*. York: Social Policy Research Unit.

Innes, A (2002) The social and political context of formal dementia care provision. *Ageing and Society*, 22, 483–99.

Ivory, M (2008) Self-directed care, individual budgets, In Control: The wider agenda. *Community Care*, 6 June.

Joint Committee on Human Rights (2007) *The human rights of older people in health care*. London: Parliamentary Joint Committee on Human Rights.

Joint Improvement Partnership South East (2010) *Reablement Review*. Surrey: Improvement and Efficiency. South East.

King's Fund (2008) *Paying the price: The cost of mental health care in England to 2026*. London: The King's Fund.

Kinnaird, L (2010) *Let's get personal – personalisation and dementia*. Edinburgh: Alzheimer Scotland.

Kitwood, T (1997) *Dementia reconsidered: The person comes first (Reconsidering ageing)*. Buckingham: Open University Press.

Knapp, M, Prince, M, Albanese, E *et al*. (2007) *Dementia UK: The full report*. London: Alzheimer's Society.

Laing and Buisson (2009) *Annual survey of the UK market for care of older people*. London: Laing and Buisson.

Lightfoot, T (2010) *Increased awareness and uptake of direct payments and personal budgets. Final evaluation and lessons learned*. Essex: Joint Improvement Partnership.

Lord Chancellor's Department (1997) *Who decides: Making decisions on behalf of mentally incapacitated adults*. London: The Stationery Office.

Luengo-Fernandez, R, Leal, J and Gray, A (2010) *Dementia 2010: The economic burden of dementia and associated research funding in the United Kingdom*. Oxford: Alzheimer's Research Trust.

Lyman, K (1989) Bringing the social back in: A critique of the biomedicalization of dementia. *The Gerontologist*, 29 (5), 597–605.

Macer, J (2011) Talking mats: Training for care home staff. *Journal of Dementia Care*, 19 (1) (January/February), 37–39.

McLeod, B and Mair, M (2009) *Evaluation of city of Edinburgh council home care reablement service*. Edinburgh: the Queen's Printer for Scotland.

Manthorpe, J and Iliffe, S (2009) Changing the culture of social work support for people with early dementia. *Australian Social Work*, 62 (2), 232–44.

Manthorpe, J and Moriarty, J (2007) *Models from other countries: Social work with people with dementia and their carers*. New York: Dementia and Social Work Practice.

Marshall, M and Tibbs, M (2006) *Social work and people with dementia: Partnerships, practice and persistence*. London: Policy Press.

May, H, Edwards, P and Brooker, D (2009) *Enriched care planning for people with dementia: A good practice guide for delivering person-centred care (Bradford Dementia Group Good Practice Guides)*. London: Jessica Kingsley Publishers.

Mental Health foundation (2008) Available at: www.mentalhealth.org.uk/content/assets/PDF/training-and-dev/dementia-choices-project-summary.pdf (accessed April 2012).

Mental Health Foundation (2011) *Personalisation and dementia: A practitioner's guide to self-directed support for people living with dementia*. London: Mental Health Foundation.

Mental Health Foundation (2012) Dementia (online) Available at www.mentalhealth.org.uk/help-information/mental-health-a-z/D/dementia (accessed January 2012).

Mental Welfare Commission for Scotland (2011) *Standards of care for dementia in Scotland: Action to support the change programme*. Edinburgh: Scottish Government.

Milne, A, Hamilton-West, K and Hatzidimitriadou, E (2005) GP attitudes to early diagnosis of dementia: Evidence of improvement? *Aging and Mental Health*, 9 (5), 1–7.

Ministry of Justice (2008) *Mental Capacity Act 2005: Deprivation of liberty safeguards: Code of Practice to supplement the main Mental Capacity Act 2005 Code of Practice*. London: The Stationery Office.

Moniz-Cook, E, Elston, C, Gardiner, E, Agar, S, Silver, M, Win, T and Wang, M (2008) Can training community mental health nurses to support family carers reduce behavioural problems in dementia? An exploratory pragmatic randomised controlled trial. *International Journal of Geriatric Psychiatry*, 23, 185–91.

Moore, D (2009) *A guide to dementia care*. Brighton: Emerald Publishing.

Moore, D (2010) *Explaining Alzheimer's and dementia – more than memories*. Brighton: Emerald Publishing.

Moore, D and Jones, K (2011) Making personalisation work for people with dementia. *Journal of Dementia Care*, 19 (1), 26–28.

Morgan, K (2009) Risks of living with Alzheimer's disease: A personal view. *Journal of Adult Protection*, 11 (3), 26–29.

National Audit of Dementia (2011) *Report of the national audit of dementia care in general hospitals 2011: Executive summary and recommendations*. London: Royal College of Psychiatrists' Centre for Quality Improvement.

National Audit Office (2010) *Improving dementia services in England – an interim report*. Press release, 14 January.

National Dementia Strategy Demonstrator Sites (2009a) *Dementia adviser services: Executive summaries of all dementia adviser sites*. London: DH Publications.

National Dementia Strategy Demonstrator Sites (2009b) *Peer support networks: Executive summaries of all peer support network sites*. London: DH Publications.

National End of Life Care Programme (2010) *Care towards the end of life for people with dementia: A resource guide*. London: National Health Service.

Newcastle Safeguarding Adults Committee (2006) *Safeguarding adults: Interagency policy*. Newcastle: Newcastle City Council.

NICE (2006) *Dementia: Supporting people with dementia and their carers in health and social care*. London: NICE.

NICE (2010) *Quality standards programme for dementia*. London: NICE.

NICE (2011) *Donepezil, galantamine, rivastigmine and memantine for the treatment of Alzheimer's disease*. London: NICE.

NICE–SCIE (2007) *Guideline on supporting people with dementia and their carers in health and social care*. London: The British Psychological Society and The Royal College of Psychiatrists.

O'Keefe, M, Hills, A, Doyle, M, McCreadie, C, Scholes, S, Constantine, R, Tinker, A, Manthorpe, J, Biggs, S and Erens, B (2007) *UK study of the abuse and neglect of older people: Prevalence survey report*. London: Comic Relief and Department of Health.

Older People's Commissioner for Wales (2011) *'Dignified care'? The experiences of older people in hospital in Wales*. Cardiff: The Older People's Commissioner for Wales.

Parnetti, L, Amici, S, Lanari, A and Gallai, V (2001) Pharmacological treatment of non-cognitive disturbances in dementia disorders. *Mechanisms of Ageing and Development*, 122 (16), 2063–9.

Pitt, V (2009) Bureaucracy restricts dementia direct payment take-up. *Community Care*, 29 April.

Rabiee, P, Glendinning, C, Arksey, H, Baxter, K, Jones, K, Forder, J and Curtis, L (2009) *The organisation and content of home care reablement services: Interim report, investigating the longer term impact of home care reablement services*. York: Social Policy Research Unit, University of York.

Riseborough, M and Fletcher, P (2008) *Extra care housing. What is it?* London: Care Services Improvement Partnership.

Rothera, I, Jones, R, Harwood, R, Avery, A, Fisher, K, James, V, Shaw, I and Waite, J (2007) An evaluation of a specialist multiagency home support service for older people with dementia using qualitative methods. *International Journal of Geriatric Psychiatry*, 23 (1), 65–72.

Royal College of Nursing (2008a) *Defending Dignity – challenges and opportunities for-nursing*. London: Royal College of Nursing.

Royal College of Nursing (2008b) *Small changes make a big difference: How you can influence to deliver dignified care*. London: Royal College of Nursing.

Royal College of Psychiatrists (2011) *Report of the national audit of dementia care in general hospitals*. London: Royal College of Psychiatrists.

Royal College of Psychiatrists Faculty of Old Age Psychiatry, in conjunction with the Alzheimer's Society (2005) *Services for younger people with Alzheimer's disease and other dementias*. London: Royal College of Psychiatrists.

Royal Commission on Long Term Care (1999) *With respect to old age: Long term care – rights and responsibilities*. London: The Stationery Office.

Sampson, EL, Gould, V, Lee, D, Blanchard, MR (2006) Differences in care received by patients with and without dementia who died during acute hospital admission: A retrospective case note study. *Age and Ageing*, 35 (2), 187–9.

Samuel, M (2008) CSCI highlight problems in councils safeguarding adults. *Community Care*, 4 November.

Scherder, EJA (2000) Low use of analgesics in Alzheimer's disease: Possible mechanisms. *Psychiatry*, 63, 1–12.

Schneider, L, Dagerman, K, Insel, P (2005) Risk of death with atypical antipsychotic drug treatment for dementia: Meta-analysis of randomized placebo-controlled trials. *Journal of American Medical Association*, 294 (5), 1934–43.

SCIE (2010) *Reablement: Emerging practice messages*. London: Social Care Institute for Excellence.

SCIE (2011a) *Protecting adults at risk: London multi-agency policy and procedures to safeguard adults from abuse*. London: Social Care Institute for Excellence.

SCIE (2011b) *Reablement: A key role for occupational therapists*. London: Social Care Institute for Excellence.

Selwood, A and Cooper, C (2009) Abuse of people with dementia. Reviews in *Clinical Gerontology*, 19 (1), 35–43.

Sheard, D (2008) See it, hear it, feel it. *Journal of Dementia Care*, 16 (5), 12–13.

Sheard, D (2011) *Achieving real outcomes in dementia care homes*. Brighton: Dementia Care Matters.

Shulman, L (1999) *The skills of helping: Individuals, families, groups and communities*. Itasca, Ill: Peacock Publishers.

Stewart, S (2006) Mental health legislation and decision making capacity: Autonomy in Alzheimer's disease is ignored and neglected. *British Medical Journal*, 332 (118), 3.

Szymczynska, P, Innes, A, Forrest, L, Stark, C, Mason, A (2010) *Best practice review: Diagnostic and post-diagnostic service provision to people with dementia and their carers with particular interest in remote and rural populations*. Stirling: The Dementia Services Development Centre.

Titterton, M (2005) *Risk and risk taking in health and social welfare*. London: Jessica Kingsley.

Tyson, A (2009) *Self-directed support: social workers' contribution*. London: In Control.

Valiyeva, E, Herrmann, N and Rochon, P (2008) Effect of regulatory warnings on antipsychotic prescription rates among elderly patients with dementia: A population-based time-series analysis. *Canadian Medical Association Journal*, 26 (5), 438–46.

Williamson, G and Shaffer, D (2001) Relationship quality and potentially harmful behaviours by spousal caregivers: How we were then, how we are now. *Psychology and Ageing*, 16, 217–26.

Williamson, T (2008) *Dementia out of the shadows*. London: Alzheimer's Society.

Wilson, V and Pirrie, A (2000) *Multidisciplinary teamworking beyond the barriers? A review of the issues*. Glasgow: The Scottish Council for Research in Education.

Woods, RT, Bruce, E, Edwards, RT, Hounsome, B, Keady, J, Moniz-Cook, ED, Orrell, M and Russell, IT (2009) Reminiscence groups for people with dementia and their family carers: Pragmatic eight-centre randomised trial of joint reminiscence and maintenance versus usual treatment: A protocol. *Trials*, 10, 64.

Zarit, SH, Reever, KE and Bach-Peterson, J (1980) Relatives of the impaired elderly: Correlates of feelings of burden. *Gerontologist*, 20 (6), 649–55.

Index

Added to a page number 't' denotes a table and 'g' denotes glossary.